THE HAUNTED
QUEEN MARY

Long Beach, California

Written by

Robert James Wlodarski and Anne Powell Wlodarski

Dedicated to:

ALL VISITORS
seen and unseen
who continue to grace the decks
of the RMS Queen Mary...

May we *all* someday rest in peace!

Happy HAUNTING from ghost to coast.

THE HAUNTED QUEEN MARY
Long Beach, California

PUBLISHED BY:
G-HOST PUBLISHING
8701 Lava Place
West Hills, California 91304-2126
Phone/Fax: (818) 340-6676 - E-mail: robanne@ix.netcom.com

Other Books Available through G-Host Publishing:
Haunted Alcatraz ($13.95)
Haunted Alamo ($12.95)
The Haunted Whaley House ($12.95)
Haunted Catalina ($12.95)

The stories appearing in this book are based on factual accounts of everyday people who have either worked on the *Queen Mary*, or who have visited the ship. The authors take no responsibility for the veracity of each story except that we believe the storytellers. Although we have made every effort to ensure that the information was correct at the time the book went to press, we do not assume and hereby disclaim any liability to any party for any loss, damage, or injury caused by information contained in this book. Furthermore, the publishers disclaim any liability resulting from the use of this book. We apologize if there is inaccurate information presented in this book, and will rectify future additions if we are contacted by mail, fax, or e-mail, and are provided with the correct information.

The authors welcome responses from our readers regarding paranormal experiences aboard the *Queen Mary*. Address all inquiries, or story submissions for future editions to **G-HOST PUBLISHING**, 8701 Lava Place, West Hills, California 91304-2126. Telephone or fax to: 818-340-6676; or E-mail to: robanne@ix.netcom.com.

ACKNOWLEDGMENTS

As for those visiting these haunted places, don't expect ghosts to appear on demand as if they are on the payroll of the local tourist office. But if you are psychically gifted—and nearly everybody is in varying degrees—chances are you may have a true experience, ranging from a psychic impression of past events to a full-blown apparition or visitation from the resident wraith. If that happens, enjoy it and don't panic. Send good thoughts to the entity you see or feel present, and go on remembering, as my good friend, the great late medium Eileen Garrett once put it, "It's such a short distance from here to there."

Hans Holzer, **Ghosts of Old Europe** (1992)

Due to all of the correspondence we have received since our first printing in 1995, we have been able to compile enough stories to complete a second edition. We are extremely grateful to those individuals who took the time to fax, e-mail, or phone us with details about their encounters including: Nick Allen, Lorraine Atkins and Tracey, John Barton and Kim Holland, Julie Bond and Sean Syfers, Elizabeth Borsting, Angela Rose Cramer, Laure DeVicenzi, Jared Fossum, Angel Gomez, Angela Guidi, Susan Hogg, Marc Horwitz, Joan Kokocinski, Rose Mejia, Cheryl Mortensen, Nery Pagella, Jane Park, Kathleen Maher-Redmond, Lisa Sather, George Stearman, Alan Thomas, Sandra Wilson, Janice Young, and those who wish to remain anonymous.

Our gratitude is extended to those who assisted in making this book on the afterlife a reality in this life. Foremost, we would like to thank Matthew and Henrietta Wlodarski for their continued support of our spirited endeavors; also, to: Mr. Joseph Prevratil, President of the RMS Foundation, Inc., for his support and belief that this book would add to the legacy of the Queen Mary; Ron Smith, Exhibits Coordinator and Archivist, for his tireless efforts to obtain valuable archival photographs, providing constructive comments, and ensuring the historical accuracy of the book; and to Stephanie Wright, Martha Chacon, and Tom Toomey for their valuable assistance along the way.

Our deepest thanks to our friend, colleague, and renowned ghosthunter, Richard Senate of Ventura, California, author of Ghosts of the Haunted Coast (1986), Haunted Ventura (1992), The Haunted Southland (1994), co-author of A Guide to the Haunted Queen Mary (1995 - op), Ghost Stalker's Guide to Haunted California (1998), and Ghosts of the Ojai (1998)—his help has been invaluable, and greatly appreciated. Richard Senate also graciously allowed us to use the Carlo Giovetti seance which originally appeared in his book, The Haunted Southland.

We are indebted to Jane Gilbert, for her valuable input.

Thanks also to Michael Massoud of M&M Printing, Woodland Hills, California, for all his help in typesetting and printing this book.

And last, but certainly not least, thanks to Matthew and Henrietta Wlodarski, Debbie Christenson Senate and Richard Niederberg, and our families and friends.

ABOUT THE AUTHORS

Robert James Wlodarski

Born in Los Angeles, California, Mr. Wlodarski has a broad-based educational background with B.A.'s in history and anthropology and an M.A. in anthropology from California State University, Northridge. The President of the Historical, Environmental, Archaeological, Research, Team (H.E.A.R.T.) since 1978, Wlodarski has managed and administered over 300 archaeological and historical projects for a variety of federal, state, county, city, and private sector agencies and companies.

Mr. Wlodarski, the President of Mayan Moon Productions, is currently developing a syndicated television series about the paranormal. Wlodarski has authored and co-authored over twenty articles for journals, quarterlies, and magazines throughout California and the Southwest. He has co-authored seven screenplays: The Crawling Eye, Cities of Stone, The Cool Change, Illusion, No Innocents, Ghost Glass, and The Palace of Unknown Kings, and has served as a Technical Consultant for Catalina, A Treasure from The Past for Ironwood Productions. Additionally, Mr. Wlodarski co-founded G-Host Publishing Company and has co-authored and published: A Guide to the Haunted Queen Mary, Ghostly Apparitions, Psychic Phenomena, and Paranormal Activity; Haunted Catalina, A History of the Island and Guide to Paranormal Activity; The Haunted Alamo, A History of the Mission and Guide to Paranormal Activity, The Haunted Whaley House, A History and Guide to the Most Haunted House in America; Haunted Alcatraz: A History of La Isla de los Alcatraces and Guide to Paranormal Activity; Southern Fried Spirits: Haunted Restaurants, Taverns and Inns, and; Dinner and Spirits: A Guide to America's Most Haunted Restaurants, Taverns, and Inns.

Anne Powell Wlodarski

Born in San Antonio, Texas, Ms. Wlodarski is a registered art therapist. She received her M.A. in behavioral science from University of Houston. She has published several articles including a chapter in California Art Therapy Trends. She has been an exhibiting artist and is the president and founder of HEARTWORLD Arts Center for Children, a non-profit organization for abused and disadvantaged youth. Ms. Wlodarski served as an education outreach coordinator and gallery assistant for the City of Los Angeles's Artspace Gallery from 1989-1993 and has been featured in the media for her work with children and the arts. She has been honored as a "Sunday Woman" by the Daily News and was a J.C. Penney Golden Rule Award nominee. She is also a member of the Daughters of the Republic of Texas (DRT), the Southern California Art Therapy Association (SCATA), and the American Art Therapy Association (AATA).

Ms. Wlodarski is Vice-President of Mayan Moon Productions, and has co-authored six- screenplays: The Crawling Eye, Cities of Stone, The Cool Change, Illusion, No Innocents, and Ghost Glass. She is currently co-developing a syndicated television series and co-founded G-Host Publishing Company. Ms. Wlodarski has co-authored and published: A Guide To The Haunted Queen Mary, Ghostly Apparitions, Psychic Phenomena, and Paranormal Activity; Haunted Catalina, A History of the Island and Guide to Paranormal Activity; The Haunted Alamo, A History of the Mission and Guide to Paranormal Activity; The Haunted Whaley House, A History and Guide to the Most Haunted House in America; and Haunted Alcatraz: A History of La Isla de los Alcatraces and Guide to Paranormal Activity; Southern Fried Spirits: Haunted Restaurants, Taverns and Inns, and; Dinner and Spirits: A Guide to America's Most Haunted Restaurants, Taverns, and Inns.

Rob & Anne Wlodarski

TABLE OF CONTENTS

It's easy to dismiss ghosts in the warm summer daylight or under the lights of a well-illuminated mall, its quite another thing to walk a dark and deserted ghost town at midnight, or creep through a dusty century-old adobe at one in the morning armed only with courage, coffee, and a flickering flashlight. Ghosts do exist! They wait behind the darkened streets and shadowed forests. They drift, ready at any time to remind us that the past isn't dead, only sleeping in that twilight between this world and the next.

Richard Senate, **Ghost Stalker's Guide to Haunted California** (1998)

INTRODUCTION

Welcome aboard the Haunted *Queen Mary,* where you can step into the past, and easily imagine what it must have been like to sail aboard this luxurious ocean liner. Memories abound throughout the ship, conjuring up nostalgic reminiscences of a bygone era.

The skeleton of Job 534, Clyde River, Scotland

The lure and magic of the *Queen Mary* is as strong today as it was when Job 534 was completed. On September 26, 1934, an estimated crowd of 200,000 people braved the cold winds and intermittent rains at the John Brown & Company shipyard on the Clyde River in Scotland to hear His Majesty, King George V, and Her Majesty, Queen Mary, usher the famous ship into history.

Launching of the Queen Mary before 200,000 people

King George V addressed the large and anxious crowd with the words, "Today we come to the happy task of sending on her way, the stateliest ship now in being... alive with beauty, energy and strength." Stepping aside, her Majesty, Queen Mary, followed by saying, "I am happy to name this ship the **Queen Mary.** I wish success to her and all who sail in her." With those words, her Majesty pressed a button which launched Job 534, the **Queen Mary,** then the largest ship in the world, into history. However, the most prophetic words were uttered by the psychic Mable Fortescue- Harrison, who boldly predicted that the **Queen Mary** would know its greatest fame and popularity when she never sailed another mile and never carried another paying passenger.

HISTORICAL INFORMATION

The Royal Mail Ship **Queen Mary** had a long and illustrious career. Generally speaking, her time at sea can be divided into three periods: The Early years from 1936 to 1939; The War years from 1940 to 1946; and the Post-War years from 1947 to her last voyage in 1967.

Her early years began with her maiden voyage on May 27, 1936, as the prize of the Cunard Line. She carried 1,742 passengers (708 in First Class; 631 in Second Class; 403 in Third Class); a crew of 1,186 men and women; 100 reporters; 6,124 sacks of mail, and during her maiden voyage, the BBC installed a number of microphones aboard ship to broadcast the event around the world. In addition, three telephone operators were in place to handle the 600 telephone receivers which were located in the First Class cabins, as well as on the ship's decks. The passengers had the novelty of being able to ring each other on board, as well as calling home while at sea.

The **Queen Mary** sailed to New York from England in four days and fifteen hours, receiving a tremendous welcome upon her arrival in the United States. Mayor Fiorello La Guardia greeted the ship at Pier 90 on the Hudson River along with other dignitaries and throngs of curious New Yorkers.

Shortly after the **Queen Mary's** maiden voyage, the quest for the Blue Riband was on; this distinction going to the ship with the fastest transatlantic crossing. Although the Cunard Line denied that it was inter- ested in the competition, it was well- known in the industry that being the fastest ship had a direct effect on passenger sales, and therefore, profits.

The **Normandie** held the record, which it set on its maiden voyage in 1935. Prior to the **Normandie,** the Riband was held by the Cunard Line from 1907 to 1929, due to the efforts of the Mauretania and **Lusitania.**

From 1929-1935, the Blue Riband was held by the **Bremen**, a German liner, her sister ship the **Europa**, and the Italian liner Rex. In August 1936, the **Queen Mary** recaptured the Riband for the Cunard Line from the **Normandie,** by traveling the distance in a record three days, twenty- three hours and fifty-seven minutes, with an average speed of more than 35 miles per hour. However, the battle for fastest ship continued back and forth with the **Normandie** until August 1938, when the **Queen Mary** once again claimed the record using a new propeller to enhance its performance. The **Queen Mary** would not lose the record again for 14 years, when, in 1952, the **SS United States,** a lighter ship with technological advancements, claimed the prize.

Life on board the ship for First Class passengers was a slice of heaven, as they were afforded every conceivable luxury and convenience. The crew and staff were highly trained to cater to the needs of everyone on board. The chefs were experts in their field, hired from some of the finest restaurants in the world. The dining salon had the largest floor space and seating capacity, and by square feet, was the largest room ever built within a ship, measuring 143 feet in length, by 118 feet in width (by cubic feet, the **Normandie** was larger). By historical standards, the three ships Christopher Columbus used to discover the New World could have been placed inside the dining room, along with the Cunard's first steamship.

Marion Davies in a First Class stateroom

Bellboys preparing for quests

Stood end to end, the *Queen Mary* was less than 229 feet shorter than the Empire State Building, taller than the Eiffel Tower and Washington Monument, and over twice as tall as the Pyramid of Cheops. Her height, from the keel to forward funnel, is greater than Niagara Falls. Recreation space aboard the ship is equivalent to a large football stadium. The main engines could generate a total of 160,000 horse power, which would equal the pulling-power of 40 large locomotives. The refrigeration needs of the ship would be equivalent to that of 15,000 tract homes. Her anchors equal the weight of 20 automobiles. She contains ten miles of carpeting, 700 clocks, and 600 phones. Over 500,000 pieces of glassware, china and table silver were used on board, along with 21,000 table cloths, 30,000 bedsheets, and 210,000 towels. Over 15,000 bottles of wine and spirits were stored in the wine cellar; and the interior decor was fashioned out of 56 of the world's finest and rarest woods. No wonder it was dubbed the "stateliest ship afloat."

A number of celebrities sailed aboard the *Queen Mary,* including: Fred Astaire, Greta Garbo, Bob Hope, Gloria Swanson, Elizabeth Taylor, Clark Gable, David Niven, Loretta Young, Marion Davies, Buster Keaton, Mary Pickford, Laurel and Hardy and many more. Prominent figures also included the Baron and Baroness de Rothschild, the Duke and Duchess of Windsor and the Vanderbilts.

Left Side: Liberace, Bob Hope, Marlene Dietrich, Fred Astaire
Right Side: Laurel and Hardy, Clark Gable, Spencer Tracy

By the time the *Queen Mary* reached New York on September 4, 1939, Hitler had invaded Poland, and World War II had begun, ushering in a new era for the ship. The British government requisitioned the *Queen Mary* for service, giving her a new coat of gray paint and converting her to a troop transport. She set sail for Australia in 1940, and, in May, boarded 5,000 Australian soldiers.

During her war years, she transported over 800,000 troops as well as passengers and refugees. She used her superior speed and maneuvering tactics as well as night-time black-outs on board to elude German U-Boats. She was well- equipped for fending off potential air strikes, carrying: Five, 40mm anti-aircraft guns, located on the bow, stern and above the bridge; twenty-four 20mm machine guns, which were located in strategic positions on the ship's upper decks; six, three-inch guns; a number of .50 and .30 caliber machine guns; and four sets of electrically fired anti-aircraft rocket launchers with twin cradles for holding 20 rockets each, which were adapted for high-angle and low-angle targets.

Additionally, special sound-detection sonar was installed to help anticipate the presence of German U-boats. Unfortunately, the noise from the ship's massive propellers made the sonar equipment all but useless. The *Queen Mary* was a "marked" ship by Adolf Hitler who offered $250,000, as well as instant hero status, to any U-Boat commander who could sink her. Her destination points included India, Australia, South America and Africa.

Prime Minister Winston Churchill made numerous trips aboard the *Queen Mary.*

Sir Winston Churchill, Walter S. Gifford and Anthony Eden

He once said, "Built for the arts of peace and to link the old world with the new, the Queens (*Mary* and *Elizabeth*) challenged the fury of Hitlerism... to defend the liberties of civilization. Vital decisions depended on their ability to continuously elude the enemy, and without their aid, the day of final victory must unquestionably have been postponed. To those who brought these two great ships into existence, the world owes a debt that will not be easy to measure."

Although the ship was fortunate enough to escape the enemy during the war, it was not exempt from tragedy. October 2, 1942, while sailing off the coast of Ireland, the *Queen Mary* accidently struck her escort cruiser the *HMS Curacoa*, literally slicing it in half. Three hundred-thirty-eight sailors out of a crew of 439, died at sea as a result of the tragic incident.

On June 20th, 1945, she arrived in New York with 14,777 American soldiers. Her tour of duty was not complete until she served for nine months as a transport carrier for American servicemen during 1946, carrying 18,900 wives and children to New York.

After being converted back to passenger service, she began her true post-war service on July 31, 1947. Gradually, with the advent of other, more improved and time-saving modes of transportation, including jet aircraft travel, she was sold. After 1,001 transatlantic crossings; three million miles at sea; transporting over two million passengers including 800,000 troops during World War II; and surviving being "marked" by Adolf Hitler, the *Queen Mary* arrived in Long Beach on December 9, 1967, after her final transatlantic voyage. At exactly 12:07 p.m., John Treasure Jones, the *Queen Mary's* last captain, announced the end of one career for the Queen of the Seas, and ushered in another—as a tourist attraction.

During the War Years, aboard the ship, politicians and world leaders made command decisions while soldiers awaited their orders below deck in cramped, stifling and claustrophobic conditions. The ship was a troop transport dodging Hitler's U-Boat commanders through the Pacific during World War II. It carried prisoners of war as well as dignitaries. They all shared the same metal frame, yet for the most part, the people on board were as different as night and day, separated not only by the decks, but by social class as well.

In its heyday, the *"Queen"* was a microcosm of society, where people from all walks of life—royalty and the working class; the young and

Crowded conditions during the War Years

the old; and people of all nationalities—sailed together. Those who worked the steaming boiler rooms, and moved about in the dark, confined themselves to the shaft alleys, barely glimpsing the light of day during their long voyages, to keep the vessel in top shape and at full speed, so those above deck could relax and enjoy the "good life."

First Class Dinning Room

Permanently docked at Pier J at the south end of the Long Beach Freeway, the **Queen Mary** is listed on the National Register of Historic Places, attesting to its unrivaled past and expert craftsmanship. The ship contains the Hotel Queen Mary with 365 restored original First Class staterooms; offers award-wining dining; contains over 85,000 square feet of multi-function space, 50,000 square feet of exhibition space; and provides tours which illuminate its illustrious history. The history of the **Queen Mary** is detailed in: *The Official Pictorial History of the Queen Mary; The Factual Story of a Great Ship R.M.S. Queen Mary Super Pictorial*; and *Gray Ghost: The R.M.S. Queen Mary at War*, available in the ship's gift shops.

Queen Mary docked at Pier J in Long Beach

A DOOR TO ANOTHER WORLD

It is no wonder, with this kind of legacy, that strange and unexplainable things continue to happen within the metal frame that holds this ship and its memories together. Sometimes it can be seen, while other times it can be heard or felt. For those who have witnessed the events, it is all too real. It is part of the oftentimes fearful unknown, a "dead zone" that sends a shiver up people's spines, makes their hair stand on end, or causes them to seek the safety of a well-lit room and find comfort in other human contact. These occurrences continue to happen with great frequency to people from all walks of life—skeptics and believers alike. As some parapsychologists suggest, where there are so many memories and emotions, there is bound to be *residual energy,* and a potential for hauntings.

With this book in hand as you take a guided or self-guided tour aboard the **Queen Mary,** you can become a part of a very special journey into the unknown; and maybe, "if the spirit is willing," you will be given a first-hand opportunity to experience a **Queen Mary** ghost.

Please be aware that when you proceed with your own ghost tour, there are several areas on the ship which are not accessible to the public. The diagrams of the ship provided in this book, illustrate areas where sightings have occurred, as well as areas which can be reached by way of a self-guided tour, and which areas can be accessed by the ship's tour.

Skeptics attribute the multitude of phenomena to natural causes, overactive imaginations and to events and circumstances which have a basis in scientific explanation. But the people who have witnessed the strange events aboard the **Queen Mary** have no doubts or illusions about what happened to them, or what they experienced. They know that something from another plane of existence, a ghost, or "energy" crossed their paths. But why?

A QUESTION OF BELIEF

The age-old questions remain: Do we survive death? and, if so, why do some choose to remain here? If we do survive, does the spirit or some form of energy remain locked in time and space, or to fulfill a specific purpose? Does a ghost represent a remnant energy from an unresolved tragedy—residue from an event that continues to repeat itself, waiting for justice or resolution, and a way to end the cycle? Are they unhappy souls looking for help—messengers or angels from another level trying to help us overcome our fear of death or save us from an impending tragedy? Or, do they willingly remain in a given space because of pleasant memories, returning to a particular place at a point in their lives when they were happy and at peace?

Perhaps this energy, or what some people call the *"spirit" or"* a *"ghost,"* represents a little of all these things: Happiness, sadness, lost souls, or angels. Maybe it is not necessary to see in order to believe—although for some it is the *only* way they will. Could it be that some of the people we see in everyday life are ghosts, quickly passing us by, only to disappear in the blink of an eye? What about those dark shadows and the cold spots which defy logic and rational explanation—and the feelings of uneasiness (or happiness) many of us have felt when we entered a place for the first time? Maybe they are ghosts!

Of all the uncertainties that exist, ghosts and the afterlife remain one of the most mysterious and intriguing. The concept defies logic, eludes scientific explanation and escapes absolute proof, yet is an integral part of our belief system. It has become an obsession for many to prove as well as disprove the concept of life after death. There has always been a deep regard and fascination with the subject that will continue long after we have left this physical plane.

Ghosts have played an important part of the history of this planet, connecting life to afterlife though myth, folklore, legend and custom. Every culture and its members have shared a personal or collective conscious experience with regard to the spirit world and ancestor worship. These experiences have ranged from love and honor, to fear and horror. Therefore, in the past, the presentation of information associated with these phenomena has been reflected in both a comedic and horrific fashion (the former possibly as a means of minimizing the frightening potential associated with the unknown).

The concept of ghosts and apparitions may have to do with the laws of the universe and gravity—the grounding of our spirit and our energy in this plane of existence; what we refer to as physical reality. The body dies, but not the spirit. It sometimes lingers, or "hangs around," so to speak. Perhaps it remains out of familiarity, or because of an addiction to a certain place; or out of repetition of old habits and patterns. As the saying goes, "old habits die hard."

Perhaps the energy we associate with a ghost cannot find its way home to a higher plane, to the light. They remain, some unhappy or confused, choosing to stay behind to watch over loved ones to deliver messages, or possibly to warn of impending disaster. Whatever the reason, that some form of energy remains, is well-documented and cannot be ignored.

THE GHOST STORIES

The stories of strange phenomena aboard the *Queen Mary* began surfacing almost immediately after the ship docked at Pier E in 1967 (later moving to Pier J in February 1971). Workers and security personnel began telling tales of ghosts roaming the decks of the ship. Whether these mysterious occurrences happened aboard the ship while it was still at sea, is mere speculation. However, there is every reason to believe that the same spiritual energy that exists now has been there all along; it simply wasn't discussed openly during that time.

Main staircase on the Queen Mary

Initially, the Wrather Corporation and Disney, early owners of the *Queen Mary,* were reluctant to admit the fact that "strange and unexplainable things" were happening aboard the ship, or to discuss the subject of ghosts. Apparently, there was some apprehension that ghosts and public relations would not mix; that the public might not accept the fact that they might have to share space with otherworldly passengers. Fearing that rumors of ghosts would spread and detract from their business by driving away potential tourists, the subject was hushed. The only stories told were related in secrecy among the staff, security guards and other personnel, who continued to witness strange events of an unknown origin.

A Haunted Corridor

Gradually, however, this mentality changed. No doubt with the advent of movies and books dealing with similar topic matter, and the dawning of the "New Age," another level of awareness was slowly fostered. The reluctance of the past gradually softened to ambivalence, followed by the realization that people were genuinely interested in, and curious about the paranormal. No doubt this coincided with the changing political and social climate around the world. People were tired of secrets being kept by politicians and the military, and were reluctant to trust the establishment and their "pat" answers.

In addition, the race for space spawned such topics as UFO sightings and abductions, crops circles and the paranormal. Finally, movies like *The Exorcist, The Entity, The Amityville Horror, Ghostbusters and Poltergeist* came face to face with *Roswell* and *Project Bluebook*. The afterlife, out-of-body experiences and ghosts were being discussed openly. Our quest for the rediscovery of the spiritual side of life was attempting to catch up with our pursuit for material satisfaction. The conservatism of this period was being replaced by the more liberal curiosity associated with looking within ourselves to find the answers to questions pertaining to our ultimate purpose in life: Why are we put here? Are we alone in the universe? What happens to us after we die? The search was on to find answers to these and other important questions, because we were facing the reality that our world was not a kind and peaceful place; that war, hatred, disease and death were all around us, and our very existence was being threatened.

For whatever reasons, paranormal investigations and psychic research were beginning to attract new followers. People seemed to be more tolerant or open to the possibilities of an afterlife. Maybe there was more to life than what met the eye. Individuals could talk about therapy sessions and channeling sessions without being completely ridiculed. One could have a personal trainer, therapist, psychic and astrologer, while discussing it all over steamed vegetables and bottled water.

An amazing shift in consciousness; a kind of spiritual renaissance was occurring. It was during this time that the owners of the *Queen Mary* began to realize that ghosts were not so bad for publicity after all. People were willing to pay to tour the corridors after midnight in search of the unexplained.

The *Queen Mary* is not the first ship to be haunted, and it certainly won't be the last. A ship that has traveled so long and so far, and has carried so many people to so many places, has countless memories stored within the rooms and corridors of its massive metal framework. There are cold spots, phantom gusts of wind, objects moving or disappearing and unexplainable electrical problems. One can hear the clanking of chains, oil drums banging and footsteps echoing in the darkness. Some people hear glasses clink and laughter ring out in the dead of night, perhaps as part of a continuing party from a bygone era.

Others who frequented the ship, or passed away on board, may not have fared so well. The good old days of parties and celebrations, also witnessed times of pain and sorrow. Who are these documented "lost souls" wandering aboard the ship? Let's find out!

JOHN PEDDER

The ship's log for Sunday, July 10, 1966 documented the following incident: At 4:00 a.m., a man was found trapped in a water-tight door.

At 4:07 a.m., the door was opened from the bridge. Within seconds, the life of 18-year-old John Pedder came to an abrupt end aboard the **Queen Mary**. Within a short time after his death, he become the most famous ghost on the ship, and has been given the nickname "The Shaft Alley Spectre." Ship's records further documented the incident by providing statements from the crew who found Pedder, crushed by mechanical door number 13 in the engine room.

According to Chief Engineer, T. Kirk, after coming on watch, he was informed by a Mr. Burgess that an accident had occurred at approximately 3:55 a.m. Fireman/ Cleaner John Pedder had been found trapped by number 13 water-tight door in starboard forward tunnel, receiving severe injuries from which he subsequently died. At the time of the accident, the vessel was in fog and all water-tight doors in the Boiler and Engine Rooms were closed on Bridge control.

When the area was examined and tested by the Chief Engineer, at 7:15 a.m, the water-tight door (horizontal type) was found to be in good working order, taking six seconds to close the maximum distance of three feet. There was no oil observed on the plates in the vicinity of the door, and the area was well-lit.

John Pedder joined the **Queen Mary** March 30th 1966. He had been engaged for three voyages as Fireman/Cleaner in the number 3 Boiler Room, and was making his 2nd voyage on bilge pumping duties in the Engine Room and Tunnels. First Junior Second Engineer, Stewart Roland Dunstan, stated for the records, that on the morning of July 10th, 1966, David Roger Cripps, Refrigerator Greaser, came to the Aft Engine Room platform and told him that someone was caught in number 13 water-tight door.

Where John Pedder died

(Photograph byRobert Wlodarski)

Keith Pilkington, Engineer on fog stand-by, hastened to the water-tight door after a phone call was made to the Forward Engine Room briefly explaining what happened. Upon his arrival at the scene, Dunstan stated that Mr. J. Hambly and Mr. K. Pilkington and himself released the trapped man, with Mr. Hambly keeping the door open while he and Pilkington moved the injured man away from the door. The Night Nursing Sister, called earlier by the Forward Engine Room, arrived a few minutes later and examined the injured man.

The First Senior 6th Engineer, J.H. Hambly, entered the tunnel, and immediately saw the trapped man in the door. Mr. Pilkington then held the man while Hambly opened the door. The injured man was then laid flat on the metal plates (the flooring) with as little movement as possible. Mr. Dunstan arrived and Hambly put a call through to the hospital, but they had already been informed.

Keith Pilkington, Third Junior 6th Engineer, added that since he was the first to reach the door, he could see that someone was trapped in it, with his back to him. Both the man's forearms were pinioned against his ribs by the door which shut crossways. Furthermore, the person was in a standing position with his head and shoulders through the door. Realizing the need for immediate action, Keith Pilkington operated the door release, but was unable to stop the person from falling forward through the door, where the body lay without sound or movement. Mr. Hambly took control of the water-tight door while he maneuvered the body clear of it. By this time, Mr. Dunstan had arrived, although they could all see that there was little hope for the man.

Angela Miller Jones, the Nursing Sister, was on duty when the call came. She had the Night Telephonist call Dr. Morgan, then hurried to the scene and examined John Pedder. She noted that there was no pulse palpable, and that he was cyanosed (turning blue due to lack of oxygen). There were multiple bruises over his arms and chest and he had been bleeding from both nostrils. No signs of life were present. When Dr. Morgan arrived, he ordered an intra-muscular injection of morphine, which Ms. Jones administered. The body was then transferred to the ship's hospital, and identified as John Pedder by David Cripps, the Refrigerator Greaser.

The surgeon, Dr. P.R. Morgan arrived on the scene at 4:10 a.m. Upon examination Pedder appeared to be dead, but because of the noise and vibration, and the position in which he was found, adequate examination was difficult. Pedder was given an injection of morphine and removed to the ship's hospital. On examination, no signs of life were detected. There were marks of a crushing injury on his arms, chest and pelvis, more marked on the right than left; there was some bleeding from the nose; no eye reflexes, and no external sign of injury to the head. There was no evidence of injury other than as consistent with his having been trapped in a water-tight door.

The 18-year-old Fireman/Cleaner from Skipton, Yorkshire, met his death trying to squeeze through a water-tight door that closed in less than six seconds. Why did he take such a risk on a routine drill? Was he playing a deadly game of "chicken" with another crew member for money, as some have speculated? Whatever the reason, his restless spirit is often seen or felt near the door that took his life.

Perhaps someone, someday can communicate with him to find out what really happened; why he remains trapped in Shaft Alley; and possibly set his spirit free.

WILLIAM ERIC STARK

Senior Second Officer W.E. Stark has been spotted in his quarters, as well as on deck on a number of occasions. Like John Pedder, Stark represents another victim of a senseless tragedy. The ship's records detail the cause of his accidental death.

According to the Staff Captain, Stark completed his night rounds and reported to him at 2200 hours on Sunday, September 18th, 1949. Stark said that he had taken a drink of tetrachloride and lime juice, mistaking it for gin, and treated it as a joke. Earlier that evening, before going down to dinner, the Staff Captain told Stark to take the two Watch Officers (after they had come off watch) to his cabin and help themselves to some gin. From there, it appears that Stark asked Stokes, the Captain's Steward, to find the bottle of gin in the absence of the Staff Captain's Steward.

Stokes went into the Staff Captain's cabin, and from a locked compartment, produced a gin bottle. The young Steward had no way of knowing that the bottle contained fluid used for cleaning cloth material, since there was no marking to show otherwise. He handed the capped "gin" bottle to Stark, and left the quarters. Stark proceeded to pour three gin and limes into the awaiting juice glasses. Unable to wait for the other officers to join him, Stark took a mouthful from one of the glasses.

*Ward Room where William Stark would most likely have
consumed the lethal dose of carbon tetrachloride*

When the other officers arrived, Stark treated the matter humorously and expected no ill consequences. However, he did telephone Dr. O'Mera, the ship's doctor. Stark informed the Staff Captain that he had not smelled the fluid because he had a cold at the time. No one thought that Stark would take a turn for the worse. It wasn't until the next day that he felt ill, and called in the Doctor, who recommended that he rest. On Tuesday, the Doctor advised his transfer to the Hospital. Stark's condition worsened with every hour, until he lapsed into a coma and died from the effects of the poison.

According to Officer Sheehan and Junior Second Officer Wicksteed, Stark seemed very jovial after coming out of the Staff Captain's cabin, where they ran into him. He told them, as he was laughing, that he had accidently drunk carbon tetracloride. Neither of the men realized the seriousness of the situation.

According to Stark, he couldn't understand why the gin and lime did not mix, the lime juice settling on the top, but he dismissed it since he could not smell. He noticed something was wrong when he swallowed the drink, remarking that it tasted pungent, and knowing that it was not gin. No one took it seriously because Stark down-played the whole thing. By the time he was taken to the hospital, it was too late. He died less than four days after accidently swallowing the poison on Thursday, September 22, 1949.

A number of unanswered questions remain: Why didn't Stark seek immediate treatment? Why did he joke to his fellow officers, knowing that he had just swallowed poison? Why didn't anyone insist that he report immediately to the Doctor? Why didn't the Doctor hospitalize Stark immediately? The poisoned officer, his life cut short by this tragedy, apparently remains in familiar surroundings, re-enacting his walks along the deck as part of his job; possibly looking for answers to why his life was cut short so cruelly; or maybe wishing to find someone to share a shot of good gin.

ENGINEER IN A BOILER SUIT

The spectre of a man in a white boiler suit has been seen and heard on numerous occasions below deck. He has been described as being in his forties and dressed in the type of uniform worn by engineers and mechanics in the early years of the ship. Does the mystery man remain on board to repeat his duties which ensured the smooth functioning of the *Queen Mary?*

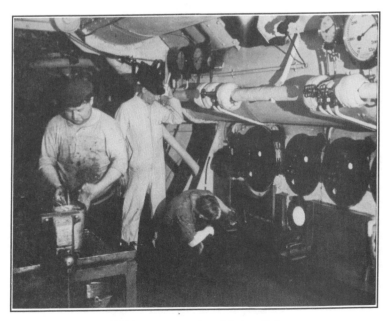

Maintenance men at work below deck

MAN IN THE OVERALLS

A man in blue-gray overalls, represents yet another spectre that has been spotted below deck. The unearthly vision belongs to a man with jet-black hair, and a long beard, who is dressed in blue-gray overalls.

His appearance is similar to the man in the white boiler suit; possibly another member of the maintenance crew who toiled away below deck. Many times, these workers braved trying conditions to maintain the proper functioning of the *Queen Mary.* He may be continuing his maintenance duties aboard ship, and repeating many of the same patterns and habits he performed while he was alive.

MINI-SKIRTED WOMAN

The poolside spirit of a young, attractive woman in a miniskirt, is sometimes viewed walking down the stairs leading to the pool, and then vanishing behind a pillar. The woman in the miniskirt is not documented in the ship's archives as someone who died in the pool area. However, she may represent someone who died aboard ship who enjoyed spending time in the pool area, where she returns to re-enact a fond memory; or, possibly a guest who died elsewhere, yet decided to come back to a place of peace and contentment while alive.

The haunted pool area where several apparitions have been reported

21

COOKING UP A TALE OR TWO

Another presence is felt or observed in the kitchen area of the ship. There are several stories which may explain the reason for the occurrences, although two of the stories represent variations of the same theme.

The basic pattern centers on the death of the cook as the result of a fight which broke out during the war years. One story suggests that a certain cook was more interested in feeding the passengers than the crew. As time passed, the crew grew to resent his attitude toward them. After months of the cook's culinary slights and lack of consideration for their needs, several of the crew reportedly tossed him into the oven.

Another account involves a potential mutiny among the American troops being transported aboard ship, resulting in a fight in the kitchen, whereby the cook, who was the object of the crew's ire, was pushed into the heated oven. He died from the resulting burns. The spirit of the cook appears to continue to haunt the kitchen area, possibly still upset that the crew turned on him so viciously. His antics can be heard, seen and felt according to many witnesses. (There is no evidence in the archives to document that such a tragedy actually took place.)

Another possible explanation for the kitchen hauntings, is verified in the ship's archives, and involves a cook named Leonard "Lobster" Horsborough. After serving the *Queen Mary* for 15 years, he died on November 13, 1967 (the *Queen Mary's* last voyage), of complications from a heat stroke and eventual heart failure. He was subsequently buried at sea by Captain Treasure Jones. Although no formal notice was given to passengers of his funeral service, a crowd gathered on the open part of "A" Deck. As word spread, morbid curiosity brought more people to view this solemn event. His remains were given up to the sea, but the circumstances surrounding Horsborough's burial may not have pleased him, considering the lack of respect during his final departure.

Since the event, tales continue to be told of the haunted kitchen area. Perhaps it is the spirit of the cook who was said to have burned alive. Then again, it may be "Lobster," who remains on board the ship he loved. If the *Queen Mary* was his world, and that world was coming to a close, perhaps he decided to exit in flesh, but remain in spirit, cooking and filling orders for other phantom guests.

Main Kitchen area where ghostly sightings have been reported

CARLO GIOVETTI - P.O.W.

Lieutenant Carlo Giovetti, an Italian fighter pilot, and prisoner of war, may have died on board the **Queen Mary.** His spirit was contacted during a seance described later in this book, coming through in a mixture of English and Italian. According to the seance, Carlo had been flying a **Fiat CR42** biplane fighter over North Africa when he was shot down by British pilots. The resulting crash caused extensive injuries to his legs.

As a prisoner of war, he was put aboard the ship, bound for Australia. He witnessed many men die while he was a captive, but could not remember the exact details of his own death. During the seance he described himself as being encased in a canvas bag and being very cold (probably the result of being buried at sea).

The results of the seance, as well as documentation obtained from England, and the ship's archives may provide substantiation to the seance. The ship's archives provide a brief reference to an Italian P.O.W., Faustino

Filippini, who died on the ship on April 17, 1943, and was buried at sea. Could this be "Carlo Giovetti?"

Research also turned up information in the form of a letter from an Italian P.O.W. who survived the war and returned to the ship in the late 1980s. The survivor states that he boarded the **Queen Mary** in May of 1941 at Suez and was taken to Sydney, Australia. He believed his group to be the first Italian P.O.W.'s to be carried in the **Queen Mary.** The P.O.W.'s were loaded aboard in cargo nets and hoisted on deck. They had hammocks to sleep in, and were only allowed on deck after the ship left port. No duties were assigned while on board, due to the poor physical condition of the P.O.W.'s. Their clothing and shoes were ragged and torn, and they were not issued new clothing until after they arrived at the P.O.W. camp in Australia. It was a stifling voyage. This information corroborates Giovetti's seance story regarding the conditions afforded P.O.W.'s aboard the **Queen Mary.**

The Queen Mary as a troop transport

Additional data suggest that many Italian and German P.O.W.'s died during transport, their bodies buried at sea. Giovetti, if that is his real name, probably died on his way to a P.O.W. camp, his spirit apparently tied to the **Queen Mary.** Perhaps the memory is so unpleasant that he cannot

24

break loose from it; or, he simply wants his story told before he can move on.

MISS TURNER

The friendly spirit of a Miss Turner also came through in a seance. According to the account, she was a freckled, auburn-haired woman, in charge of the 700-line switchboard located on "B" Deck. It was the largest switchboard installed on an ocean liner. It became immediately apparent on the maiden voyage that she was in way over her head.

Main swithcboard in operation—the spirit of a former operator was contacted during a seance

According to historical records aboard the **Queen Mary**, there were so many calls to and from the ship during her London-New York crossing, that a number of them were never able to be placed. An inspection of the Ship's records, do not list the names of all personnel on the maiden voyage. Therefore, verification that a woman named Turner worked the switchboard is still lacking. Why she remains on the ship is anybody's guess—perhaps to complete the backlog of unfinished calls, or continue as operator for the spirit world.

MRS. KILBURN

The spirit of a Mrs. Kilburn also came through in a seance. She was described as being trim in her gray uniform with starched white cuffs, and very efficient. She was in charge of the stewardesses and bellboys during the voyages. Going to sea was nothing new to her, since her family had served the Cunard Line for three generations.

Kilburn was a nurse and schoolmistress before joining the staff aboard the *Queen Mary.* A strong-willed woman, and stickler for detail, she demanded efficiency and neatness from her staff. Her philosophy was very simple: Smile if you want; otherwise be efficient. As with Miss Turner, there has been no verification, as yet, of either her name on the crew manifest, or her death aboard ship. Perhaps Mrs. Kilburn remains to make sure everyone puts his/her best foot forward!

THE LADY IN WHITE

Although there is no historical documentation available about the Lady in White , she is frequently seen in spirit aboard ship. She appears to have haunted the Main Lounge (now the Queen's Salon), and was seen

Main Lounge: The favorite haunt for the Lady in White

from time to time waltzing into the Lounge wearing a backless, white evening gown. As the stories went, she either strolled over to the grand piano as if listening to a ghostly rendition on the keys, or danced by herself for a few moments before vanishing into thin air in front of startled witnesses.

An interesting twist to the story involves the grand piano. Several years back, the piano was moved from the Main Lounge, to Sir Winston's Piano Bar. Although the Lady in White ceased showing herself in the Lounge, she has begun appearing at Sir Winston's. Apparently, as the piano moved, so did the Lady.

The spirit of the Lady in White represents one of many such phenomena seen aboard the ship. These manifestations may be residual energy resulting from an actual death where a spirit returns to a specific location due to fond memories, to repeat certain behaviors; or, as in the case of the Lady in White, become attached to a specific object—the grand piano.

OTHER ACTIVITY ON BOARD

A number of other incidents of paranormal activity have been reported over the years by security guards, staff, crew and paranormal investigators. In fact, security on board have often been troubled by the doors aboard the ship which appear to have a mind of their own.

For unknown reasons, doors that are locked one minute, mysteriously become unlocked the next, triggering alarm lights in the security office. This occurs most frequently with the doors near the swimming pool. Inspections have been unable to turn up any culprits, but someone or some THING appears to be playing tricks on them.

Numerous other accounts of strange phenomena, include: inexplicable noises, such as the sound of footsteps when no one is there; banging and hammering, as if someone is working on long-since removed equipment; voices; enigmatic cold spots and winds in air-tight areas; lights going on and off of their own accord; and objects disappearing, or being moved—the list continues to grow!

WHO'S COUNTING

Historical sources place the death toll aboard the *Queen Mary* at

55, since it was launched in 1936. Of the 55 documented cases, 39 were passengers and 16 were crew. The ages range from a child who died at birth, to a 77-year-old woman, The deaths have resulted from: Heart attacks; people jumping overboard; falls; an overdose; accidental poisoning; being crushed to death; and natural causes.

An area where two guests reportedly fell to their deaths

Psychic investigators believe that the death toll may actually be in the hundreds, if the deaths of P.O.W.'s are considered. During the war years, because the ship was used as a troop transport as well as carrying prisoners of war, unconfirmed stories tell of suffocating heat below deck, resulting in frequent deaths and burials at sea. Finally, though accidental, the **Queen Mary** was involved in the sinking of the **HMS Curacoa** on October 2, 1942, resulting in the deaths of 338 seaman. According to the records, while the **Queen Mary** approached the Scottish coastline with 10,000 American troops aboard, she came in contact with a small destroyer escort which intended to protect the **Queen Mary** from submarine attack, if it became necessary. Leading the entourage was the 450-foot-long, 4,290-ton British anti-aircraft cruiser, the **Curacoa.** Tactical procedures called for the destroyers to form a protective cordon around the **Queen Mary.**

Suddenly, before anyone realized the danger, the **Queen Mary,** still on her usual zig-zag course as a matter of standard wartime operating procedure, hit the unsuspecting **Curacoa** at high speed. The force of the

Queen Mary impacting the *Curacoa,* 150 feet forward of the cruiser's stern, spun the ship broadside to the *Queen Mary's* bow, which sliced the *Curacoa* in half, like a stick of butter. Many of the *Curacoa's* crew died instantly below deck, drowning in the cold seas as the ship sank.

Two crewmen were able to make their way to safety from below deck by crawling into a hatch leading into one of the vessel's funnels. They reached the side of the sinking ship, and slid down her hull into the icy water.

The crew and soldiers on the upper decks of the *Queen Mary* could only watch in horror as the *Curacoa* went under. Some of those who watched, had the sensibility to begin throwing life preservers to the stranded men below. The *Curacoa* sank in less than five minutes. The *Queen Mary* radioed for help, but could not risk the lives of 10,000 men by attempting to rescue the remaining survivors, and was forced to continue on. Sixty-two of the 400 men aboard the *Curacoa* miraculously survived the collision.

The *Queen Mary,* though suffering damage to her bow, managed to make it to port without further incident. Perhaps a few of the victims of the Curacoa remain attached to the *Queen Mary,* seeking retribution— since a wartime investigation laid one-third of the blame for the accident on the *Queen Mary* personnel.

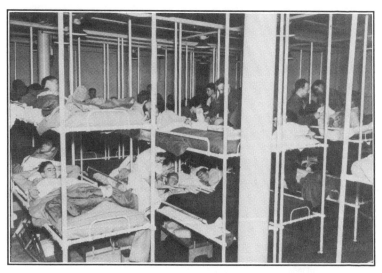

The Pre-War Main Ballroom was fitted as a troop hospital

There are those, including historians and psychics, who feel that the men who worked or were forced to occupy the space well below deck, sometimes suffered great hardship due to the intense heat and emotional flare-ups. In addition there are indications that the prisoners of war may have been occasionally mistreated while being transported during war time. Apparently, while at sea, a few of those who died were kept in a make-shift morgue aboard ship, their bodies refrigerated until the ship reached port. Others were buried at sea.

GUEST GHOST SIGHTINGS

Over the years, many guests have responded to the haunting questions of mysterious happenings aboard the *Queen Mary* by filling out questionnaires or sending in letters which documented their experiences. These responses in the ship's archives have produced some very interesting information, which follows:

T.L.G. AND R.B. OF CALIFORNIA - At eleven p.m., we went to our room, B123, located next to the Coke machine. As we entered, we saw a man standing by our bed. He was about 5'11" tall, broad- shouldered, and wearing a black, navy coat (porter/pea coat) and a black cap. He remained for a few seconds and then disappeared, We were not frightened as much as caught off guard. We remained in the room, and he came back to visit one more time. We have no idea was he was doing there, or what he may have been looking for.

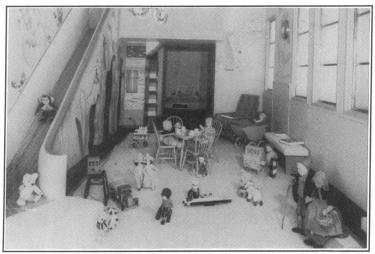

The Haunted First Class Nursery

L.S. OF CALIFORNIA - My friend and I, while on the guided tour, which included the nursery area, heard a noise at the door to the nursery, that the guide couldn't open. It rattled by itself and made clicking noises. Also, several times during the tour, I felt as if someone was constantly tugging at my purse and shirt, even though no one was standing next to me. Another time, I had the strongest feeling that I was being followed in one of the hallways. Later on during the tour, as I was standing at the end of the line, and the air was completely still, I felt something touch my hair. It gave me the chills since I looked around and there was no one to be seen.

H.H. OF DELAWARE - While taking the tour, I stopped at the pool and decided to toss a penny in for good luck. As I was throwing the penny I heard what seemed like someone whispering to me, telling me that it was not nice to throw things in the pool. It was a distinct sound that seemed to pop inside my head. I looked around, and no one else could have said it.

S.N. OF CALIFORNIA - While I was staying in Room A138, I heard a knock at the door. When I opened it, there was no one there. I looked down the hall, and it was deserted. I thought I was hearing things. However, later that night it happened again. There was a faint knock at the door which I went to check on. Again, there was no one at the door or in the hallway. It was a very strange feeling.

L.B. OF OREGON - My family and I were on the bridge looking around. I wandered off by myself to the chart room.

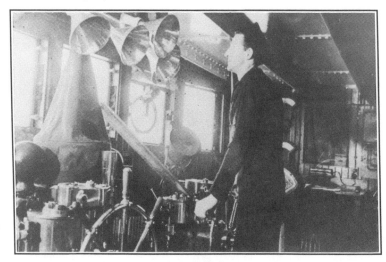

The Haunted Bridge

As I was finding the *Queen Mary* on a map they have in the room, I had the sensation that someone was tugging at the back of my shirt. Thinking it was a family member, I turned quickly, and felt a chill. There was no one around. I left the room at once, with goosebumps all over my body. This was the first time anything like that ever happened to me.

M.H. OF OHIO- Last night I was awakened from my sleep by the sensation that the ship was pitching or rolling. I do not drink, so I couldn't attribute it to that. I am familiar with traveling at sea, and being that the ship is protected from the open sea, and that the water was stable all week, it couldn't have been caused by currents. I reasoned that maybe I was taken back in time to when the ship was at sea. I couldn't explain it any other way.

H.H. OF CALIFORNIA - While exploring the sun deck by the elevators, I heard the distinct sound of footsteps running up the stairs. Then, out of the corner of my eye I noticed that the porthole at the top of the stairs had suddenly gone dark and it looked as if rain was beating against the glass. As I heard the footsteps coming closer, I turned away from the porthole toward the sound, but no one was there. When I looked back at the porthole, it was normal once again. The experience gave me butterflies in my stomach. After that, I had a strong desire to go to the Engine Room, even though I had never been on the ship before. It was as if I was being led there by some force.

G.F. OF OREGON - After visiting water-tight door number 26, I saw the back of a man in dark blue work clothes walking through a narrow hallway. He didn't look like he belonged on the ship, so I attempted to follow him. I looked everywhere, but I never found him, or anyone who looked like him.

J.M. OF CALIFORNIA - I was at the Purser's Desk when I caught a brief glimpse out of the corner of my eye, of someone or something moving. It was there for a second, and then it was gone. I looked around, but could not find anything. I was positive that it was not my reflection, but I don't know exactly *what* it was.

C.L. OF CALIFORNIA - At the Sundeck exhibit, beyond the stairwell heading down, I got a mental image of a male between 20-25 years-old, wearing a blue mechanic's uniform. After a few seconds, the feeling left me and the area felt cold and empty.

D.D. OF CALIFORNIA- In the pool area, I saw a huge puff of steam rise from nowhere. As quickly as it appeared, it diminished. Right after that, I saw a small girl across the pool. I asked about her, but apparently I was the only one who saw her. She had dark hair, and was wearing a white and blue dress with a square collar and puffed sleeves. She looked like a hologram image that just disappeared in front of me. I'm not sure anyone else saw it.

P.M. OF TEXAS - I awoke from a deep sleep to the sound of snoring coming from the other side of the bed where my husband was sleeping. At first I thought it was him, so I listened. He was quiet and asleep. I heard the snoring again, and this time I woke my husband up. He dismissed the entire incident and went back to sleep. But, I did hear *something* on the other side of me, and it wasn't my husband.

J.M. OF CALIFORNIA - While touring the Sun Deck exhibit area, I noticed a middle-aged lady near the piano. She wore a brown dress with a white lace collar, and a light green sweater, with a gold pin. I turned my head for a second, looked back, and she had vanished. I don't know how she could have gotten inside the exhibit and then out so quickly. I'm positive it wasn't my imagination.

D.G. OF CALIFORNIA - My friend and I were alone on the top deck. We went downstairs to the deck below, and heard footsteps as if coming from a large group of people on the deck where we had been. Since we didn't recall seeing anyone on that deck prior to going down, we decided to go up and check. As we looked around, we got the chills. The deck was empty!

I.G & M.G OF CALIFORNIA - We stayed in Room A110. When we checked in, I distinctly remember leaving our luggage on a chair, away from where we walk. Later that night, when I went to the bathroom, I tripped over my luggage. Somehow, after going to bed, our luggage had been moved several feet from its original position, blocking access to the bathroom. My wife denied moving it, but *someone* did.

A.C. OF CALIFORNIA - I awoke from a deep sleep around midnight. I saw a figure walking near my daughter's sleeping bag toward the door. Thinking it was my sister, I called out. There was no answer. It was then that I noticed my sister was lying next to me. I sat up in bed and watched the person in white walk through the door! I was unaware at the time of the ship's ghosts.

V.G. OF CALIFORNIA - I stayed in Room M029, and would like to relate two curious events which took place while I was on board. While I was shaving, my kit fell off the shelf in front of the bathroom sink. No one else was in the room at the time, and I examined the shelf closely—it was straight and quite secure. The second incident occurred when I was drawing the bath for my wife. I couldn't budge the faucet. My wife tried to help, but both of us couldn't turn the water on. Trying one last time, the faucet turned on easily.

Strange occurrences have been reported in several bathrooms

A.F. AND C.F. OF VIRGINIA - We stayed in room B462. As my husband was brushing his teeth, he felt a tightening in his chest, as well as the sensation of someone watching him. When he came into the bedroom, he saw a lady between 25-35 years-old standing near our baby. She had brown hair and was wearing a long, white camisole-type gown. When I looked again, she had vanished.

LOCATION OF SIGHTINGS ABOARD THE QUEEN MARY

Access Legend

W   -   Walking tour - self-guided
LA -   Limited access: part of ship's tour
NA -   Not accessible

Sightings Legend

1. Sports Deck - Sir Winston's Piano Bar: LADY IN WHITE {W}
2. Sports Deck - MISS TURNER [W]
3. Sports Deck - WILLIAM STARK'S room [W]
4. Sports Deck - The haunted Bridge area [W]
5. Sun Deck - The haunted exhibits area [W]
6. Promenade Deck - Original sighting of the LADY IN WHITE [W]
7. Promenade Deck - Main Ballroom [W]
8. Main Deck - Likely spot where passengers viewed LEONARD HORSBOROUGH'S burial at sea [W]
9. Main Deck - Children's Nursery [NA]
10. "A" Deck - Location of the "Old Spice" encounter [W]
11. "A" Deck - Likely spot where LEONARD HORSBOROUGH was buried at sea [W]
12. "A" Deck - Location of a haunted stairway [W]
13. "B" Deck - Male and female hospital rooms [NA]
14. "R" Deck - Main Kitchen area [NA]
15. "R" Deck - First Class Main Dining Room [LA]
16. "C" Deck - This area served as the ship's morgue [NA]
17. "C" Deck - The ship's hospital area (male and female ward rooms) [NA]
18. "C" Deck - Catwalk overlooking the Boiler Room [W]
19. "C" Deck - The haunted pool area and dressing rooms [LA]
20. "G" Deck - The haunted Engine Room and Shaft Alley [W]
21 "G" Deck - Water-tight door number 13 [W]
22. "G" Deck - Boiler Room encounters [NA]

*** Several hotel rooms on the Main Deck, and "A" and "B" decks are reportedly haunted

SPORTS DECK

SUN DECK

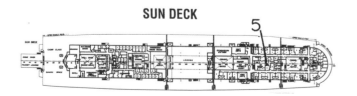

PROMENADE DECK

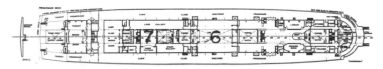

MAIN DECK

"A" DECK

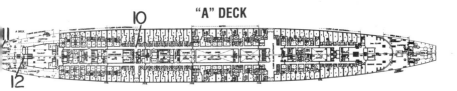

"B" DECK

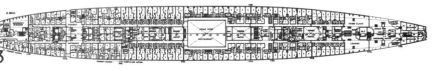

"R" DECK

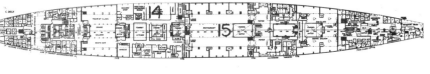

"C" DECK

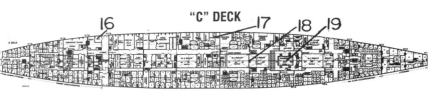

"G" DECK

C.S. OF CALIFORNIA - While I was walking on a self-guided tour, I approached water-tight door number 13. I heard someone whistling, and went to look for the source. I checked all around, but I couldn't find where it was coming from. There was no one down there except me, Also, near emergency steering in the Engine Room, I heard someone running, but I could not locate a soul. Something strange is happening below deck.

S.S. OF CALIFORNIA- Out of the corner of my eye, I saw a man in a blue shirt, walk toward a long hallway. As I turned to follow him, he vanished into thin air. He looked like he didn't belong there.

H.V. OF CALIFORNIA - I was awakened from my sleep and observed the image of a person standing in front of my bed. There were no apparent physical features, but it appeared to be holding a flashlight, with a light shining out of it that was brighter than the form itself. I watched as the image swayed back and forth. When I called my roommate, the vision backed up. I called again and the vision backed up even further, toward the door. I reached for the light switch and tried to turn it on. The light switch seemed to spark and wouldn't turn on all the way. Finally, my roommate woke up; the light came on, and whatever it was, was gone. We slept with the TV on the rest of the night. It was a great experience, and I had a lot of fun!

A typical first class room

S.M. OF OREGON - I was in the pool area and saw a tall woman dressed in an old wedding gown. Her hair was in a bun and she was with a nicely-dressed boy in a suit. It sent chills down my spine, because as quickly as they appeared, they vanished into thin air! I know I was not hallucinating.

P.T. OF CALIFORNIA - I was alone in Shaft Alley near water-tight door number 13. I decided to talk to John Pedder, because I heard his story and felt sorry for him and the way he died. I told him how lonely it must have been to die by himself. As I stood in the middle of the door, and moved back and forth a few times, I saw something move out of the corner of my eye. It was a brief glimpse of someone or something, maybe John. I did not feel threatened, nor did it make me fearful. To be honest, it was not the first time something like this has happened down there. I have had a similar experience before.

E.B. & B.B. OF CALIFORNIA - We spent the night in Room B401. While we were relaxing, we both heard taps or a light knocking on our suite door. I asked who it was, but there was no reply. I got up to open the door, and when I looked out, there was no one to be seen. This happened later on that night with the same results. Maybe it was someone playing a practical joke, although I think we knew it was something else.

M.F. OF CALIFORNIA - While on the ship, my husband and I occasionally joked about someone following us, or of hearing a thumping sound coming from below. Actually, if we would have been confronted by anything out of the ordinary, we probably would have been frightened. When we went through water-tight door number 13 in Shaft Alley, knowing the story of John Pedder, we jokingly asked him if he would like to join us on our little self-guided tour. When we were leaving the ship I noticed that my husband had a spot of black grease on his face, as if someone put the tip of their finger up against his face and pressed. We could never figure out how the grease got there. Maybe John left his calling card!

 ** If, after *your* visit aboard the *Queen Mary,* you have a story to tell about a strange or unexplainable experience, please fill out the attached form at the back of this book.

WALKING TOUR INTO THE UNKNOWN

 Several ghost-hunting tours have been conducted on the *Queen Mary* since the late 1980s by Richard Senate, a professional paranormal investigator, and his wife, Debbie Christenson Senate, a psychic. Excerpts from some of the participants who attended one of these tours, provide insights into the phenomena observed and/or noted aboard the ship. They also represent the impressions of average people who spent a rather harrowing night aboard the ship in search of its ghosts.

Because this was a special ghost tour, the participants were al-lowed in areas of the ship which are not normally accessible to the public. The diagrams of the ship presented within this book, illustrate areas where sightings have occurred. They provide information as to which areas can be reached by way of a self-guided tour, or the ship's guided tour. Note that some areas are inaccessible to the public.

TOUR GUEST # 1

As we walked through the Captain's cabin, I had the strangest sensation of getting seasick, as if the ship were moving. It got so bad, I had to leave and go outside for fresh air. Once I went outside, I felt better.

Another situation occurred while I was walking through the Main Ballroom area. When I walked inside, I came face-to-face with a cold spot or cold front in one area of the floor. All around me the air was warm, so it was hard to explain why this one place was so cold. I checked for drafts or air vents and found nothing that would explain the sensation.

There was also a room where I felt very lonely at the end of the crew quarters, portside of the big hole. In addition, the catwalk above the boiler room scared me, and I am not afraid of heights. Finally, I got chills when I entered the Boiler Room, and at the center, below the catwalk.

TOUR GUEST # 2

There were several areas we visited as part of the tour, where I felt uneasy. One place was the pool area, which kind of spooked me. In particular, I had a very heavy and weighty feeling when I passed through the pool dressing rooms, and in general, when walking around the pool area. Another area which felt "unearthly" was in the First Class bathroom. I wanted to leave the minute I walked inside.

TOUR GUEST # 3

While on the tour we went to the pool area which was very eerie, especially by the women's bathroom. I felt a chill like I'd never felt before. The changing room, especially, feels very active.

The eerie Dressing Room in the pool area - Some psychics consider this to be the gateway to another dimension

While I was wandering through the ship's artifact display area, which at one time was either part of the engine room, or where a smoke stack once was, something poked my friend. Maybe there is [a ghost] there because all the old items from the ship are on display.

Finally, when we got back to our room on board the ship at 4:00 a.m. I sat on my bed with the dowsing rods, and felt a spirit in my room—a woman between 15-25, whose name began with the letter "J." She was friendly and I felt her presence with us in the morning.

TOUR GUEST # 4

While walking through the pool area, I saw a girl standing there, as clear as day. She appeared to be from the 1940s, and seemed to be cheerful and content. My feeling is that this person once sailed on the **Queen Mary** as a young lady, maybe in her early twenties, and after dying, many years later, comes back to a time when she was happiest, and very carefree.

Sketch by eyewitness

She is mischievous, and sometimes likes to play hide-and-seek with people rather than trying to frighten them. I sense that she is there all the time, watching and waiting, giggling behind a pillar. She's excited that so many people come to visit the pool area to see her.

TOUR GUEST # 5

When the tour group visited Shaft Alley at 3:30 a.m., dowsing was very active by two different doorways. One was where John Pedder died. We thought we heard footsteps by the door. The guard who was with us said he had never *seen* a ghost, but the he has *felt* John's presence.

TOUR GUEST # 6

While walking around the pool area, each time I looked from the guide to the pool, I noticed a red light in the same place. On the catwalk over the boiler room, I waited until most of the people were off the bridge before I crossed. I felt something nudge me; it felt like a ripple going up my spine. The whole boiler room was very creepy, and I felt like I was not wanted there. I felt very unsettling things on the Promenade, as if something was just not right. I was tired and drained being in that area of the ship.

TOUR GUEST # 7

When I walked through the doors to the pool area, I got chilled. My whole body shook—there is definitely something there! I also got a sad feeling when we went to the boiler room, and heard strange noises. There are many areas where you feel uneasy, as if you are constantly being watched.

TOUR GUEST # 8

I did not feel comfortable in the Boiler Room. When I visited the pool area, I was overwhelmed by a sense of hardship, fear and strife, as if people had lived there in crowded conditions and several had died. As I walked around the pool, the name Julie Aura came into my head. I sensed that she drowned, and her body was found unclothed. I felt that she was 24-25 years old, and had either traveled in Second Class with her aunt, or had an affair with and older, married man in First Class, where they met late at night by the pool. [There is no substantiation in the ship's archives of any person drowning].

TOUR GUEST # 9

I felt a tightness in my chest when I passed through the dressing room area by the pool. A sadness came over me there—someone crying perhaps? I felt the same sadness and pressure on my chest in shaft alley.

TOUR GUEST # 10

It was exciting to participate in the seance. I enjoyed the entity of Clara that came through Debbie. I felt so much pity for her—she was so naive. Toward the end of the seance, I felt a sharp pain, a pinching on my neck, which hurt me. I called out to the others. The name Sarah Longwoods came to my mind, and I called her name. It was a wonderful experience.

TOUR GUEST # 11

Upon entering the pool area, I was immediately drawn to the steps on the left, where I felt a strong sense of dread and anxiety. When I went down the stairs, I stood at the corner of the pool. While standing there, I experienced the same feelings I had upon entering the pool area. I also felt a cold spot over to the side. There was a strong feeling coming from the room under the stairs. In the dressing room I had a strong negative feeling at the very end in the shower and toilet room.

Entering the boiler room, I felt something at the first railing, and saw a strange haze between a beam and the wall. After that, I walked around the room, then came back to the same railing, but the feeling wasn't quite as strong.

Strange sounds continue to be heard in the Boiler Room

In the Officer's Quarters, I felt something in the chained-off hallway. I walked over to the area, and felt a cold spot in and above the chair closest to the exit. It seemed as if there was someone sitting and watching me.

TOUR GUEST # 12

During the seance, I sensed that there are many people, who for some reason have not realized that they have "crossed over." The Boiler Room gave me an eerie feeling when we went down there.

When we went to the pool area, I thought I saw an older woman swimming in a black, one-piece bathing suit, and wearing a white bathing cap—the name Adelle came to me.

Last night, about 1:00 a.m., after I returned to my room, I heard a moan in the bathroom that sounded like Carlo from the seance. Also, as I went to sleep, my bed appeared to be rocking gently.

TOUR GUEST # 13

The tour eventually went to the pool area. It was there that I saw a woman standing by the side of the pool. She had brown hair, and was wearing a white dress. She appeared to be petite and young. I took my eyes off of her to see if other people were watching. By the time I turned around to look again, which was only a matter of a few seconds, she disappeared.

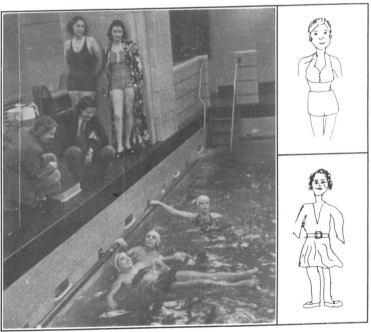

The pool area and eyewitness sketches

TOUR GUEST # 14

After the seance and the tour, I had a few impressions of the time I spent with the group. The Boiler Room seemed to be a deep, dark dungeon and a scary place to be. I learned during the seance that there were more ghosts here than John Pedder and the woman in the pool. My general feeling is that there are many souls trapped aboard the ship.

TOUR GUEST # 15

I received consistent readings from my dowsing rods of spirits in three places that we visited on the ship. The first area was in the side hallway between cabins B421 and B423; the second was in the staircase between the main deck and "A" Deck, top half, aft, starboard corner; and the third, was in the First Class pool area in the forward, starboard corner of the pool. While in the pool area with the group, I got a sudden chill on the back of my neck.

TOUR GUEST # 16

During the ghost tour, I got very negative feelings in a couple of areas. One area was located near the left-hand corner of the pool area, and the other area was in the ballroom, where I had a very strong feeling of someone watching me. There was another area in the Officer's Quarters, where it felt as if a force of some kind was blocking me near the chairs.

TOUR GUEST # 17

While we were walking in the pool area, my friend went out in the corridor and said that she felt a presence next to her. As it turned out, this corridor led to the Boiler Room. As I walked down the corridor to the boiler room, I felt a strange chill. While in the room, the silence and emptiness caused my mind to wander, allowing me to imagine what it must have looked like when the ship was in operation. I also felt something in Shaft 7, Door 13, which was the area where crew member Jonathan Pedder was crushed during a routine drill. According to tour guides, there have been numerous sightings of a man in white overalls below deck, especially in the boiler room area.

TOUR GUEST # 18

In the pool area, down below the diving board, on the right-hand side, I saw an image of a woman. As walked through the First Class Dining Room, I smelled flowers... Gardenias? In the boiler room, I heard sounds of metal hitting metal, as if men were working. I heard a man yelling, "Turn that off, damnit, turn it off!" In the Third Class Dining Room, my friend felt a presence by the piano—he sensed it was a man who resented the intrusion. My hair stood on end.

Debbie Senate felt that the presence was a male, and there was a barrier she could not break through. The image I got was of a male in his mid-40s-50s, brown hair, dark vest, open shirt, with light brown clothing.

My friend felt someone watching us in the Second Class Dining Room. Richard felt a tingling sensation in the pool area, and the tour guide reported seeing the ghost of a girl in a green mini-skirt in this same area. One member of the team saw a red light in the pool.

DEBBIE CHRISTENSON SENATE

Debbie toured the swimming pool area, and was stunned to see a red glow in one of the dressing rooms, and a figure swimming under the water. The image didn't last long. Others in the group saw bubbles appear in the water.

Phantom sounds of children playing and guests strolling have been reported on many of the decks

RICHARD SENATE

Debbie and I walked the darkened decks of the moored ocean liner. It was almost 4:00 a.m., and there was no one around. Suddenly, we heard footsteps on the deck above us. Debbie turned to me and said, "Those footsteps are made by ghosts." They seemed so real, I doubted this; and since we were close to a stairway, I leaped up the steps to confront our fellow night owls; however, there was no one to be seen—we were alone!

OTHERWORLDLY HAPPENINGS

There are literally hundreds of other stories about ghosts and paranormal activity aboard the **Queen Mary.** A few of the more unique encounters have been directly recounted or paraphrased.

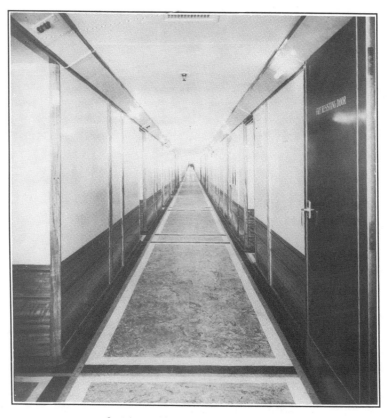

Certain corridors are reportedly haunted

A CONCESSIONAIRE MEETS AN UNKNOWN FORCE

On "A" Deck near the stern of the ship, next to a stairway, the concessionaire and his friend were walking down the corridor late one night, when they noticed a tray near one of the cabin doors. As they approached the stairway, the tray literally flew down the corridor before coming to rest 40 or 50 feet away from them. Frozen in their tracks, they felt a rush of cold air pass through them. Within seconds, a sign hanging on the corridor wall was ripped off, and flung onto the carpeting. They saw no one, and didn't wait around long enough to encounter any further activity.

THE TOUR GUIDE AND THE GHOSTLY CHILDREN

A tour guide related his story of hearing the laughter of children and the sound of footsteps on the deck above him as he was walking up the aft stairwell. The sound continued until he neared the top of the flight of stairs. The sound of laughter was such that he knew he would come across the children any moment. As he reached the top of the stairs he heard the laughter, as if they were next to him—but he was alone. After a few moments, the sound stopped as quickly as it had begun. This incident made for a rather hair-raising experience.

The ghostly sounds of children have been reported in several areas

A DOG IS MAN'S BEST FRIEND... UNTIL IT MEETS A GHOST

Another story involves a security guard with a dog patrolling "G" Deck. As they made their way along the deck, the dog stopped, snarled and began growling. As the guard urged the dog on, it began to whine, and wouldn't budge from its position. Finally, the sound of something metal rolling toward them prompted the Guard and his dog to immediately flee the area. As chance would have it, the incident took place in Shaft Alley where John Pedder was killed.

HOW MUCH IS A STORY WORTH?

A journalist decided to roam the dark corridors of the ship late one night, in search of ghosts—something he did not believe in. In the early morning hours, while being shut off in Shaft Alley by design, he heard a loud clanging sound, as if someone were banging on the pipes. When he approached the area from where the sound emanated, it stopped—when he backed away, the sound began again. As he moved away from the sound, his retreat was blocked by an oil drum which had mysteriously appeared out of nowhere. He began to panic.

The Engine Room has been the scene of frequent sightings

Trying to beat a hasty retreat, he proceeded up the passageway. Feeling his way back in the darkness, two more oil drums blocked his path. Overcoming those obstacles, he walked cautiously along a catwalk, only to encounter an ominous presence. Someone or something was coming toward him, but he couldn't see anything. After quickly shifting directions, he felt a sudden rush of wind in an airtight area brush by him. Stopping "dead" in his tracks, he heard the faint sound of men talking. No one else should have been down there. Within a short period of time, all the voices trailed off, except one. That is when he heard some unintelligible words followed by a more distinct phrase, "Turn the lights off!"

After his ordeal ended, he asked the security guard about the voices he heard. Could there have been other people below with him? The response was an emphatic "No." Apparently the closest person to him during that time was two decks away. The guard confirmed that others claimed to have heard ghostly voices in the Shaft Alley area as well. We don't know if the journalist changed his mind about ghosts, but it seems that someone was certainly trying to persuade him!

HAUNTED HOUSEKEEPING

A woman working in the housekeeping office on "A" Deck, related the story of an uncanny event which took place while she was on duty. She described seeing "someone" wearing a white dress, standing by Frame 135 elevator in the "A" Deck service area. The housekeeper was having a hectic day, and thought it was just another employee performing her routine duties, even though the woman looked odd, and transparent.

She remembers glancing away for a heartbeat before deciding to take a more thorough look. In that brief moment, the ghostly woman vanished. There were no sounds of footsteps, or of the elevator being used. The housekeeper was alone, left only with the image of the apparition.

A TALE OF TWO WOMEN

Two female guests became caught up in ghostly room encounter. While occupying Room M202, both women were awakened by the sounds of people putting clothes away in an adjoining closet. The banging and thumping were so loud, that they were about to get up to complain. Suddenly the commotion stopped, and the two women went back to sleep.

In the morning, they decided to walk by the cabin where the sounds had come from the night before, hoping to discover who the noisemakers were. What they found, shocked them—there was no cabin or closet. The adjoining area next to where they slept was open space next to the bulkhead!

The next night, again, both women were awakened. This time, by the sound of someone constantly going to the bathroom. They heard footsteps repeatedly cross their cabin floor, enter the bathroom and shut the door. They looked around but couldn't find a "living soul." One of the women refused to take a bath, saying that the faucet emitted weird sounds, and the room had an unnerving, eerie quality to it.

AN ORDER FROM ANOTHER DIMENSION

Bizarre things occur quite often on the *Queen Mary.* However, for one female employee, they happened with greater frequency. According to her, most of the strange events took place on the lower decks: Dishes flew around, she heard knocking on a table when no one was there, and tables shook while she read the newspaper.

On one occasion, in the Promenade Cafe, the employee noticed a woman dressed in 1940s clothes sitting at a coffee table. The clothes were a "dead give-away," since the 40s "retro" look was not fashionable at the time. The employee took her eyes off the oddly dressed woman for a moment, then turned back to find that she had vanished. After looking around without success, she knew "they" were playing tricks on her again!

Deserted Promenade Deck

CREW MEMBERS BELIEVE

A few years after the ship arrived from her last voyage, people began to talk secretly about strange, spooky things happening around the ship. People reported seeing shadows, hearing voices and noises when no one else was around—things no one could explain after each search for evidence proved futile.

People began reporting that they saw things around the pool area: Wet footprints, as if someone just got out of the water; a woman in white who walked barefoot by the pool and disappeared; and an angry cook who walked around slamming doors and making noises. These kinds of stories date back to the 1930s when the ship was first commissioned, and there were at least half a dozen separate sightings.

BEYOND A SHADOW OF DOUBT?

One employee who worked on the ship for a number of years, saw plenty of things that couldn't be explained, such as plates flying across the room in the cafeteria. He was positive there was a ghost in the main kitchen area. He was also matter-of-fact in stating that there are places the crew won't go because they are frightened—like the wardrobe area, where the ship's morgue was supposed to be. People say that it's eerie and cold in there. The exhibit hall seems to be another place where people hear things when no one else is around—voices and other noises.

The employee continues, talking about the lady by the pool who is there one second, then disappears. That's just one of the places the employees won't go alone. Another is the Engine Room which also seems to have its own, not so pleasant feeling. This employee is positive that there are spirits on the ship. To him, it's a matter of "live and let live." In fact, he says, "Some of the places have different feelings from others; scarier, where you get goosebumps or feel cold."

LIVING IN HARMONY WITH THE DEAD

Another employee actually *likes* the idea of spending time with the spirits. He mentioned working in the main kitchen and definitely feeling a presence keeping an eye on him. He also feels cold spots where there are no drafts or ventilation, and is firmly convinced that there are people "not of this world," watching him.

He doesn't care what people think, and he isn't afraid, saying, "People shouldn't be frightened of what they can't see. The ship has its own feeling, as if you are in another world, but you get used to it. Leave them be and they will let you do your thing."

THE TOUR GUIDE AND THE POOL GUEST GHOST

One day, while a tour guide was alone by the swimming pool waiting for a group to arrive, she spotted an elderly woman standing by the edge of the pool. The woman appeared to be in her sixties and was wearing

Another view of the haunted pool

an old-fashioned, one-piece bathing suit and bathing cap; her curly hair protruding from under the cap. There were two disconcerting problems:

The elderly woman appeared to the guide in *black and white*; and secondly, was about to dive into a pool that had no water (it had been drained). Thinking the strange-looking woman might be a tourist who accidently wandered into the pool area, the guide's immediate reaction was to call security.

Before summoning help however, the guide decided to turn and warn the woman not to jump in. In that brief moment, the elderly woman disappeared. The confused guide immediately began checking the doors— They were all locked. A thorough inspection revealed no trace of the strange-looking woman. Although skeptical about ghosts, the guide was convinced that what she saw was real. As an afterthought, she reasoned that if it *was* a ghost, perhaps it was someone who enjoyed the pool area during a cruise, and was returning to the place that brought her pleasure.

GOING UP?

Another tour guide, while closing up, was walking into the south alley where there are two sets of escalators. He was coming up one escalator, when just a few steps from the top, he had a distinct feeling that someone was behind him. Sure that he was the last person on the shift, he turned slowly to find a man standing on the escalator. The man had black hair, white skin, large, dark eyes and a nicely kept black beard. He was wearing dirty blue overalls as if he had been repairing something. He wasn't threatening, and didn't try to communicate. He just stood there quietly.

The guide turned to watch where he was going as he reached the top of the escalator, and stepped aside to let the man pass. When the guide turned, the man in the dirty blue overalls had disappeared. The guide didn't see the man appear or disappear, but in a matter of seconds, he was there and gone.

THE PLUMBER AND THE POOL PARTY

A "routine" plumbing job turned out to be anything but routine. While working the graveyard shift, a plumber on his way to the shop, which is located close to the pool, distinctly heard voices accompanied by the sounds of water splashing, glasses clinking and a ball bouncing.

His first inclination was to think that guests had made their way to the pool and were having a late-night party. However, as he turned the corner and reached the pool area, there was no one in sight; no movement in the water; and no glasses or ball to be seen. Thinking that his mind was playing tricks on him, or someone else was, he went back to work. A short time later, he heard the same sounds again. Cautiously approaching the pool area, he looked in again and saw no one. He called Security, but nothing or no one was ever found.

THE GHOSTLY ENGINEER

Another story surrounding Shaft Alley involves two couples aboard the ship. According to the story, one couple came up the escalator from Shaft Alley and reported to maintenance personnel that a man in white coveralls had told them that he had dropped his wrench, and asked them to bring him another one.

A short time later, a second couple came up the escalator with the same story for the maintenance personnel—an engineer in white coveralls told them that he had lost a wrench and needed another one. The description of the coveralls didn't match the present-day uniform, and the bizarre nature of the engineer's request from below deck caused them to investigate. There was no man to be found anywhere. He had vanished, presumably without finding a replacement wrench.

THE PSYCHIC AND THE QUEEN

Several prominent psychic investigators have visited the *Queen Mary* over the years. This particular investigation yielded some very interesting feedback regarding the ghostly population aboard the ship.

The psychic began by stating that there were "spirits all over the ship." In order, she picked up on a John (John Pedder died in 1966); the letters of another name "STAR" (possibly William Stark who died in 1949); a man named Mitchell (possibly Captain G.T. Mitchell [not a captain of the *Queen Mary*] who died in 1967 and was buried at sea); and a man named Charles, who worked on the ship, and may have died on board (Charles Summers died in 1949, on voyage 119, of pancreatitis); the name William, Williams or Bill also came through (W.M. Holden drowned in 1943; William Eric Stark was accidentally poisoned in 1949; William Earnest Humphries died from natural causes in 1950; William Henry Barrett died from a heart attack in 1950; Richard Walter Williams died in 1951; and William Henry Pope died from a prescription overdose in 1964).

Continuing, the psychic also made contact with a lady who wore a long, white dress with dark cuffs, possibly fur-lined, in the salon area of the ship. She stated, "The lady likes the ballroom where she sometimes sings and dances." She also picked up on George Gershwin or Cole Porter music, and the initial "J" (this is in keeping with other stories about a woman with a name beginning with the letter "J"). "The lady may have been an entertainer, who sat by the piano and sang, and loved the ambiance of the ship," the psychic said.

By the pool area, the psychic saw ectoplasm or a fog-like substance and picked up on a woman who may have been pushed into the pool and murdered. In the ballroom, the name Richard or Robert filtered through from the other side (Richard Rolland Metcalf died from a heart attack in 1950; John Robert Maloney died from unknown causes in 1951; and Richard Walter Williams died in 1951).

The psychic investigator stated that some spirits may come to the ship, as if drawn, because they had wonderful times aboard, and they often return to places where they experienced happiness. They represent earth-bound spirits who don't know they have passed on, and continue to repeat the same things they did while alive, going largely unnoticed. Sometimes recognition by another helps them move on; it can be verification that they are dead. When you are near a spirit, it often gets cold, and feels like you are walking through someone. The psychic concluded, "There is so much going on around us that we simply cannot or will not see, but the energy is definitely there. It is nothing to be afraid of. There is no feeling of intent to harm that I can feel on this ship."

A PSYCHIC IN THE NEWS

A recent television special featuring renowned parapsychologist Peter James, provided some startling new information about the paranormal activity on board the ship, as well as further documenting existing phenomena. The extensively researched television segment began with James stating that the **Queen Mary** is purported to have over 600 ghosts aboard the ship. He followed with a confirmation about the numerous sightings, especially in the below-deck areas, and the fact that the ship appears to be "saturated with spiritual energy."

During the segment, stories were related about the "kitchen spirit;" the ghost energy in the pool area; the restless energy where the morgue and coffin storage areas used to be; voices of children crying in the cargo

Children playing in the Nursery

hold area; sounds of footsteps of invisible people running along darkened corridors; ghostly laughter and haunting, unexplained sounds in the Boiler Room; below-deck passageways and abandoned rooms; and the voice of the spirit of a young child, who continues to cry out for her parents (recorded on tape by James).

A SECOND TIME AROUND?

A story with a very unusual twist came by way of a tour guide, who was given this information (on file in the ship's archives) first-hand, and transcribed it as follows: In 1988, the then-Assistant Manager of the

Hotel Queen Mary received a letter from a couple in England. They had sailed on the luxury liner from Southampton to New York in 1958 on their honeymoon, and wanted to celebrate their 30th wedding anniversary on the ship. They requested the same room they had occupied in 1958.

Since the room numbers had changed often over the years, the Assistant Manager had to search the records to see if the room was still in use, and if so, what the number now was. He found the room, and discovered that it was still part of the hotel. He reserved the room and wrote to the couple, assuring them that everything would be as they wished. (He had never met these people, nor spoken to them.)

On the day of the couple's arrival at the ship, the Assistant Manager was behind the front desk of the hotel. They entered the lobby, took one look at him, and froze in their tracks. They would not approach him. They would not speak to him. They would not have anything to do with him. He didn't know what was going on. Had he offended them in some way?

Eventually, the Assistant Manager went into the back office. A few minutes later, the Manager came in and told him to take the next three days off with pay. He offered no explanation. The Assistant Manager left, still not knowing what had happened. He ended up returning from his "vaction" a half-day early because someone had called in sick. He was behind the front desk when the couple came up from "B" Deck to check out. Again, they took one look at him and froze. And again, the Assistant Manager was completely baffled.

After a lengthy period of awkward silence, the woman approached him and began to explain. In 1958, each passenger was usually serviced by one particular steward or stewardess. Instead of giving them a tip every time they brought a drink or a newspaper or whatever, they were often given a chunk of money in a tip envelope at the end of the voyage. This couple had a wonderful steward while on board—great service, great attitude. They wanted to tip him when the *Queen Mary* arrived in New York; however, they couldn't locate him anywhere. He was not on the ship, and no one knew what had happened to him. Eventually, they discovered that the steward had taken ill just before the *Queen Mary* docked, and was taken off the ship to the hospital, where he died.

The couple never saw the Steward again—that is, until they ran into the Assistant Manager—he was the "spitting image" of the Steward.

The resemblance was so uncanny, that the couple was uncomfortable being around him. Even more amazing, is the fact that the Steward died in 1958, *on the same day the Assistant Manager was born!* (The Assistant Manager has since passed away, perhaps finally joining his "spirit double.")

GHOSTS WEREN'T IN HER CONTRACT

Prior to becoming an employee aboard ship, S.J.G. became a **Queen Mary** Ghost Club initiate. Her first encounter with the unknown occurred while completing what she thought was a quick contracting job aboard the ship. This is her story:

Her first encounter began after the current CEO received the lease to operate the **Queen Mary** in 1993. She was contracted to dress the windows in Piccadilly Circus before the Grand Re-opening event being planned. The previous management had closed the ship, and it was not open for business until the second quarter, 1993.

Empty corridor during conversion to a tourist attraction

Security was located in an area that is currently known as Queen's Marketplace, away from the ship. This added to her sense of uneasiness and feeling of isolation. The atmosphere was unique in terms of lighting, sound and temperature. She felt the need to work quickly, get the job done and get out. As she decorated the half-circle windows to the Kodak Shop, the *normal* ambiance seemed to give way to a completely *different* feel. "If one assumed that I was a little frightened, he would be correct," S.J.G. stated. She decided not to look around because she felt that someone was continually watching her, and wasn't particularly keen on finding out who it was. So, she concentrated on the job at hand. All she could think of was finishing her work and getting off the ship.

S.J.G. said, "It seemed as if noises were coming from all around. There was a constant *whooshing* sound as if crowds of people were moving by me. Hammering and banging noises, coming from several decks below, filled the night. At 1:00 a.m. I really wanted to leave the ship, even though I'm not easily frightened. To relieve the tension, and maybe placate whoever or whatever was there, I repeated over and over in my mind, 'I'm here making your ship very attractive, and I'm here to help, so don't hurt or scare me.' I managed to get my work finished, and never did see a ghost, but I certainly felt *something* all the time I was there."

More recently, S.J.G. had another strange encounter. Her office is located on "A" Deck, midship, portside. According to preliminary research, the office used to serve as the loading lobby for passenger luggage in the early years of the ship's operation. In fact, it still retains the sealed doors which once opened to the outside.

The first two months S.J.G. worked there, during the summer of 1995, she noticed the smell of *Old Spice* cologne outside her door near the fire extinguisher. (Her office is nestled between two hotel rooms.) The first time it happened was around 8:00 a.m. "The smell of cologne was so strong, that I assumed it must be a businessman staying in an adjacent room," S.J.G. revealed. However, there was no evidence of anyone occupying the room.

The next occurrence also took place during the morning hours, a few days later. Again, the smell was so strong, that it permeated her office. S.J.G. immediately ran out to see if she could spot someone. Glancing down the corridor, hoping to catch sight of the responsible party, she saw no one. This time she felt that the cologne belonged to an elderly gentleman because the scent was so over-powering. (The sense of smell is one of the first to weaken as people age.)

Two weeks later, after lunch, she was going back to her office, when the smell of *Old Spice* again lingered outside the entrance. I permeated the area, and she looked at the carpet to see if perhaps someone had spilled a bottle of the cologne. She found nothing. The last time this happened, she checked everywhere and was again left without a clue.

S.J.G. told us, "I figured that I may have a gentleman spirit watching over me, so I decided to accept his presence and not question the purpose of his visits. I was curious, however, and decided to have a friend research the date that *Old Spice* was originally marketed. Oddly enough, it turned out that the cologne was first manufactured in 1936, the year of the maiden voyage of the *Queen Mary!*"

SEANCE OF OCTOBER 27, 1987

Debbie Christenson Senate, a psychic, performed a seance aboard the *Queen Mary* on the night of October 27, 1987. She went into a deep trance at approximately 12:06 a.m. Eighteen people were present in a small circle. Several spirits made their presence known during the seance. The following represents an account of the event which is taken directly from *The Haunted Southland* by Richard Senate.

Debbie sat up in her chair, her eyes still closed, her face twisted in pain.

(Debbie): "My legs," she cried out, "My legs, pain."
(Richard): "What is the matter with your legs?"
(Debbie): "Pain. My legs are wounded."
(Richard): "What is your name?"
(Debbie): "Carlo."
(Richard): "Did you have another name?"
(Debbie): "Carlo Giovetti," she answered in a pained voice.
(Richard): "Are you Italian?"
(Debbie): "Si."
(Richard): "How were your legs injured?"
(Debbie): "Shot down, crashed."
(Richard): "Who shot you down?"
(Debbie): "English," She said with a sneer of hate, "English Spitfires."
(Richard): "What year is this?"
(Debbie): "1941."
(Richard): "What did you do?"
(Debbie): "Pilot, Regia Aeronotica."
(Group Member): What kind of plane did you fly?"

(Debbie): Falco, Falco, CR 42 Falco."
(Richard): "What was this plane like?"
(Debbie): Biplane, Falco is a good plane."
(Richard): Biplanes were not used that late. Are you sure it was a biplane, two wings?"
(Debbie): "Si, Falco."
(Richard): "Where were you based?"
(Debbie): "Bengali, Bengali."
(Group Member): Is that in North Africa?"
(Debbie): "Si."
(Richard): "How did you get to North Africa?"
(Debbie): "Kangaroo, I was kangarooed."
(Richard): "What is a Kangaroo? Was that the name of a ship?"
(Debbie): Airplane, Kangaroo. Falco folded up. Placed in Kangaroo. My plane was folded up."
(Richard): "Did you mean your Falco folded up and crashed?"
(Debbie): "No, no, Kangarooed. SM 82, flown to Bengali."
(Richard): "What is a Kangaroo?," I asked for a second time.
(Debbie): "Plane, three-motored transport."
(Group Member): "Your plane was folded up inside another larger plane and flown to North Africa?"
(Debbie): "Si."
(Richard): "What was your squadron number?"
(Debbie): "162-B, no, 162-A."
(Richard): "What were you doing the day you were shot down?"
(Debbie): "Reconnaissance over Bar Dee Ah."
(Richard): "What happened after you were shot down?"
(Debbie): "Captured by British. Taken to Alexandria."
(Richard): "What happened then. Did the British take care of your legs?"
(Debbie): "No. British kicked me. Placed on board the Queen Mary."
(Richard): "Where were you placed?"
(Debbie): "In the bottom of the ship. The air was hot, so hot."
(Richard): Did you see a Doctor?"
(Debbie): "The English want to cut off my legs! I won't let them. Bugs are crawling all over my legs. Make them stop!"
(Richard): "Why do they want to amputate your legs?"
(Debbie): I will never fly again. Don't let them cut off my legs."
(Richard): "What is it like on the ship?"
(Debbie): "Infantry - infantry. They placed me with the infantry men, pigs!"
(Richard): "Where were they taking you?"
(Debbie): "Australia."
(Richard): "Were there any injured men on this ship?"

(Debbie): "Many, five or six died each day. It was so hot."
(Richard): "What did they do with the dead?"
(Debbie): "Overboard."
(Richard): "Was there a priest on board? Someone to confide in, for last rites?"
(Debbie): "No priest. My legs hurt so bad. I can't feel them now. Oh mama! Oh mama!"
(Richard): "What's happening now?"
(Debbie): "They put me in a bag, a canvas bag. It's cold, the water is so cold"."

Debbie let out a scream and fell forward in her chair.

In an effort to substantiate Carlo's story, the research proved quite interesting. Archival information on file at the Imperial War Museum in London revealed that a bomber/transport, referred to as the **SM-82** (Savoia-Marchetti), was first flown in 1938. A three-engine craft, it helped supply the Italian Army in Africa, operating until 1960. The design of the plane enabled a complete **CR42** biplane to be housed, once its wings and tail surfaces were detached and stored longitudinally. At least 50 fighters were transported to Africa in this manner.

Drills during World War II

The **SM-82** was also called **Canguro** (Carlo's Kangaroo), or **Marsupiale**. When Italy entered the war, she possessed 12 of these transport vehicles, forming Squadrons **607a** and **608a** of the **49a Gruppo** at Naples.

Additionally, the **CR42** was the last biplane to be constructed by Fiat, and one of the last biplane fighters built anywhere in the world. The **CR42,** Falco (or Falcon) was first flown in early 1939, and placed in production the same year. Technological advancements in airplanes phased out the use of the Falco in 1945. Finally, the **CR42** served in North Africa, just as Carlo had said.

Other documentation corroborates the fact that voyages during wartime were indeed hellish. They were very tense and emotional. The crew and soldiers were on constant alert for German U-boats who were trying to sink the **Queen Mary**. Fortunately, her speed and evasive tactics at sea, saved her from peril. Aboard ship, the heat was oppressive, especially during the voyages to Australia and Egypt.

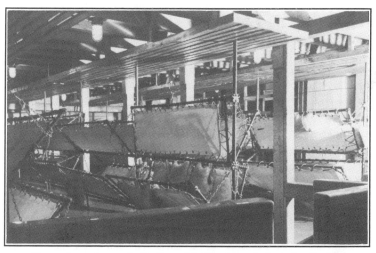

The pool area jammed with tiers of folding frame beds during the War

Without air conditioning, the decks below became floating sauna baths. It appears as if many soldiers died of heat exhaustion. Tempers flared, gangs operated below deck and threats of mutiny occurred during these voyages. Frequent salt water showers were the only relief. By November, during the time of the **Queen Mary's** final war-time run from Australia to Suez, they had delivered 80,000 Anzac troops to Egypt, while returning with many Italian prisoners-of-war for confinement in Australia.

It would appear that the story of the painful journey of an Italian prisoner-of-war, one Carlo Giovetti (though the name cannot be verified) a biplane pilot for the Italian Air Force, holds a great deal of credibility. Like John Pedder, William Eric Stark, Miss Turner and Mrs. Kilburn, Carlo has a name; however most remain nameless—for the moment.

MORE RECENT TALES

A LATE CHECK IN

A woman and her husband related a strange experience they had after checking into room M202. While asleep, they were rudely awakened at around 2:00 a.m. by a series of loud, thumping noises, as if a person or persons were walking near their closet. Suddenly, the thumping was accompanied by banging, then shuffling sounds, similar to someone unpacking. They laid in the darkness for at least a minute, listening to the noises, thinking that it must be late arrivals settling into the room next door. Finally, the noise was too much, and they turned on the light to place a call to the front desk. As they flicked the light on, the noise abruptly stopped. They waited for the sounds to return, but nothing happened. Several minutes passed, and they were able to go back to sleep. The next morning, their curiosity got the best of them, and they opened their door to see if they could catch a glimpse of their noisy neighbors. To their amazement, their was <u>no cabin</u> adjoining their room—the only thing next to them was an empty corridor!

JUST TAGGING ALONG

On one occasion, a guest reported that after checking into room M147, she quickly unpacked and decided to take a leisurely stroll above deck. After leaving her room, the woman began ascending an adjacent stairwell leading to the next level of the ship. After climbing a few steps, she became keenly aware of someone following her. The guest heard the distinct sounds of footsteps directly behind her. The footsteps were accentuated by a "creaking" sound. She stopped and turned around, thinking the person was going to pass her at any second. There was no one to be seen. Puzzled, the guest began the ascent once again. Just as before, her steps were instantly mimicked by the sound of a second person trailing her by only a few paces. Stopping again, this time to give the annoying "person" a piece of her mind, she was greeted only by an eerie silence. This time, however, within seconds after turning around, the guest felt a rush of cold air passed right by her. She had heard about the haunted reputation of the ship, but she never envisioned something like this actually happening to her!

THE INTRUDERS

A tour group had a taste of the unknown while visiting the 3rd class dining area. While the tour guide was talking, he suddenly became quiet. Within seconds, the entire group began rubbing their arms from an intense cold which had suddenly enveloped them. They all remarked that they were feeling tingling sensations throughout their bodies, followed by the hair on their arms and the backs of their necks standing on end. As they stood in front of the piano, they began discussing the fact that they felt as if they were being watched by an unseen presence, and how the room had suddenly become freezing cold. One member of the party exclaimed that she saw a man around forty, with dark hair, wearing a vest and dressed in light brown clothing standing near the piano; and he was staring at all of them! She remarked further that the man appeared agitated because the tour was intruding on his "quite time." The tour continued, but no one could stop talking about their ghostly encounter.

3rd Class Dining Room circa 1937

A DOOR TO ANOTHER DIMENSION

Although security guards are trained to react to adverse conditions, they are usually not prepared to deal with the paranormal. When it comes to the unseen, no amount of training and bravado can help them handle the situation any differently from the average person. One evening while looking in the pool area just before closing the door, a security guard felt an intense blast of cold air blow through him. He looked around, but saw no one. Not wanting to stay any longer than he had to, and reasonably sure that no one was left behind in the pool area, he closed the door and began walking away. Within seconds, he heard the door open behind him. He stopped, did an about-face, and hurried back to the door. It was now wide open, although he positively locked it moments before. Once again he felt an intense cold engulf him. Wasting little time, he quickly locked the door just as before, and ran out of the area as fast as his legs could carry him. He didn't wait to see if the door stayed locked this time.

A SPIRITED NAP

This event took place during a cold, February afternoon, and involved truckdriver J.Y. of Corona, California. According to J.Y., she checked into room B409 with a friend, and while they were both lounging around the cabin table, talking, they began to hear someone snoring in one of their beds. Stunned, they looked at one another in disbelief. Just then, the lights in the bathroom began flicking themselves on and off several times in succession. Before the two could react, the snoring ceased. However, the lights in the bathroom continued to go on and off for a few more seconds. Finally, everything was quiet. The friends were more dumbfounded than frightened at what had just occurred. They immediately got a pad and pen and began writing down the experience. They continued talking about the event for the rest of their stay on the ship. It was decided that even ghosts have to sleep!

THE POOL PHANTOMS

A female security guard received several calls one day about a couple of noisy teenagers who were playing in the first class pool area. Since this area is normally locked (except when tours are being given) to prevent visitors from injuring themselves by accidentally falling into the drained pool, everyone assumed that the kids had broken in. Checking out the disturbance, the guard stood outside the locked door for a few seconds and heard kids playing in the pool area. She immediately unlocked the door and rushed in, hoping to catch the pesky kids in the act, but the noise immediately ceased and the guard saw no one.

First Class Passengers enjoying a swim

Positive that a couple of children were hiding, the guard quietly opened one of the two gates which allow access to the pool area, then locked them so no one could escape. She performed a thorough inspection of the entire pool area, including the darkened dressing room corridor. There were no children or anyone else for that matter in the area. As the guard approached the gates to leave, one was wide open as if someone walked out while she had conducted her search. Also, the door leaving the pool area was still locked, so no one could have left the area. More than a little nervous, the guard locked up again and quickly left. If ghostly pranksters were responsible for the noise, so be it!

A CRYING SHAME

This incident took place one fall afternoon when the ship was sparsely filled with tourists. After receiving several calls from guests complaining that a baby was crying incessantly in a nearby room, security was quickly dispatched to handle the situation. After checking with the front desk regarding the room where the baby was heard crying, the security guard was surprised to discover that the room was not rented out! The guard headed for the room thinking that someone had illegally entered it with a child, hoping to spend a free night aboard ship. As the guard approached the room, he heard a child wailing, loud and clear. The guard called out repeatedly to be let in while standing outside the door—to no avail. Concerned, the guard called into the main office for permission to enter the room. After several more futile knocks, the guard unlocked the door. He wasn't sure what to expect—an abandoned child or worse. As he entered the room, the child's crying abruptly stopped. The room was unoccupied, and there was no sign of life anywhere! The puzzled guard left the room and reported the incident. Four more times during the course of the day, the crying was reported by disgruntled guests, and each time the same security guard was dispatched with the same results—an empty room. Finally, to the relief of staff and security, the crying stopped for good. No explanation was ever found to account for this strange phenomenon.

BOILING OVER

While on a scheduled tour of the boiler room, J.F. of Minnesota, and several other members of the tour group, including the tour guide, were startled when they heard the sounds of boilers running full blast. The noise was loud enough that it echoed throughout the area. Although long since dismantled, the sound was unmistakable and frightening to those who heard it. The noisy, pulsing sounds lasted less than a minute, then everything was quiet. The tour guide just shrugged his shoulders and said nonchalantly, "What do you expect on a haunted ship?" J.F. replied that the place was eerie enough without the ghostly sound effects.

KNOCK, KNOCK

During October, A.T. of Grand Terrace, California was staying in room B142 with his wife. According to A.T., they were relaxing in their beds when they heard several knocks at the door. A.T. called out for a response, but no one answered, and the knocking continued. Finally, he got up to see who was at the door. When he opened it, no one was there.

AFT turbo generating room

Thinking that someone was playing a prank on him, A.T. quickly ran into the corridor, but found no one around. He and his wife were perplexed by the mysterious knocking. Later that night, while trying to go to sleep, A.T. had an intense, frightening, feeling that someone else was in the room with him and his wife. He kept looking around the room, and could not shake the strange feeling of being watched. The next day, his wife, told him that she had felt very uneasy the entire night, as if someone else was watching them. Could the strange knocks have been from an otherworldly visitor, someone they let in, but couldn't see?

THE GHOSTS NEXT DOOR

It was around midnight, on a warm June evening when J.P., of Tiffin, Ohio, her daughter, sister and friend experienced an encounter with the paranormal as they shared a room next to the Eisenhower Suite. The weather was beautiful, and the lights glistened from across the channel as the group finished their stroll around the deck. After returning to their room they began relaxing and talking. Suddenly they began hearing loud noises coming from the adjacent suite. Although J.P. assumed that the late arrivals were unpacking, the amount of noise suggested that a group, rather than one or two people had settled in and were having a party.

War time fun

After several minutes, the noise became unbearable and J.P. began banging on the walls to try an quiet things down; however the shuffling, and unpacking sounds continued. Finally, the noise abruptly stopped. The next morning, J.P. went over to check on their noisy neighbors and made a startling discovery: The room next door was not only unoccupied, but was never used for guests. No one could logically explain who had come to party that night. Whoever, or whatever had checked in to the room, was not of this world.

CHIPS AHOY

About 9:00 p.m. one night, N.A., a ship employee, was busy working at Portside Necessities on "A" deck. He usually worked the 3:00 p.m. to 10:00 p.m. shift, and stated that nothing unusual ever happened to him while working, even though he knew the ship had quite a reputation for being haunted. Not that he was a skeptic; he was fairly confident that the spirit sightings were real, but were meant for the visitors, not the employees. On this particular evening, while N.A. was working alone, a bag of potato chips suddenly flew off the rack and onto the floor.

Surprised, he looked around to see if anyone witnessed what had just happened. There was no one else around. N.A. cautiously picked up the bag of chips, and put it back on the rack. Before he could turn around, the same bag once again flew off the rack and onto the floor, as if someone N.A. couldn't see, was having a little fun with him. N.A. was not amused. He got a little spooked at that point, but once again returned the chips to the rack. This time N.A. concentrated all his attention on the bag. This time it stayed put. The incident never occurred again.

A guest sketch of John Pedder

PEDDER FILE: THE LINE-UP

Several years after the *Queen Mary* was up and running as a tourist attraction, a young woman, while embarking on a self-guided tour of the engine room and shaft alley, had an unforgettable brush with the unknown, and the spirit of John Pedder. Although paranormal sightings and incidents were frequent after the *Queen Mary* became a tourist attraction, employees were discouraged from discussing the ghost stories for fear that it might create problems. Ghosts and spirits were not considered good for business. Late-night discussions among employees, especially security guards who were witnessing strange things on a regular basis, were the only means of communicating these events. Guards often talked about strange, phantom-like shapes, disembodied voices, unexplainable sounds, parties without people in the pool area, and trained guard dogs refusing to venture into certain areas of the ship. Guard duty, especially during the hours from midnight to six in the morning, was seldom dull, since there always seemed to be "someone else" around.

One visitor, strolling below the deck, found out what most employees already knew—the *Queen Mary* was *very* haunted. The aforementioned young woman was described as a sharp, no nonsense person who came aboard because of her love for the *Queen Mary*, and the proud history. Like many tourists, she preferred her own company to that of a tour group. As she explored what is called "shaft alley," she marveled at this metal, man-made wonder. Making her way through the maze-like catacombs that provided access to the engine room, and below deck compartments, she passed the notorious water tight door Number 13. There weren't many people wandering the corridors, so when she spotted a young man in a seaman's uniform standing at attention near the escalator, she hesitated. He looked odd, lost, with a faraway look in his eyes. His melancholy gaze passed right though her, and frightened her a little. She wasted little time passing by him, and making her way to the main deck. She couldn't forget his forlorn gaze, and sad expression etched on the man's face. Perhaps he was a maintenance man who was very tired, or just had a tragedy befall him.

When she reached the main deck, she decided to ask a security guard about the poor, lonely-looking man who was standing at the base of the escalator. The security guard couldn't remember any scheduled maintenance in that area, so he obliged the woman and went to look. He asked her to wait there until he returned. A short time later, the guard said that he searched the entire area, and found no one working anywhere who fit her description. He reiterated that there were no mechanics, repair men, or other workers in that area today. She adamantly insisted that she saw the man at the escalator wearing an odd-looking uniform. The security guard politely asked if she could describe the man she saw. Within seconds after giving her description, the guard asked the woman to accompany him to the security office. She obliged, and off they went.

While in the security office, the guard laid out a number of photographs, and asked the woman if any resembled her uniformed maintenance man. Without hesitating, she immediately pointed to one of the photographs. The amazed guard proceeded to tell her that it was impossible; the man that she said she saw, and the photograph she picked out, was a former crewman named John Pedder. Pedder, he said, sailed on one of the last cruises the **Queen Mary** took as a passenger carrier in 1966. "So, he's still working on the ship!" the woman exclaimed. The guard shook his head, and reluctantly told her that John Pedder had been killed, crushed to death, a few feet from where she had spotted him, at water-tight door Number 13.

BANG THE PIPES SLOWLY

J.B., and S.S. of Crestline, California, after having settled into room M220 for the evening, were kept up most of the night by an almost constant clanging, and banging which seemed to surround them. The noise seemed to be at its worse at 9:30 p.m., midnight, 3:00 a.m., and 7:30 a.m. The two wary guests described the sounds as workmen installing pipes or fixing the plumbing. These were not the normal sounds associated with the ship, but distinctive noises that filled their room. A check of the adjacent areas, including the rooms above them revealed no workmen, and no bizarre sounds. It was like a scene from the past, when the ship was in operation. The last noise was heard around 7:30 a.m. and then ceased for good. The couple didn't get much sleep that night, but they did take home a memorable experience.

SHAKE IT UP, BABY

During late May, J.B., and K.H. of Hesperia, California, while staying in room M140, were treated to an event that really shook them up. While taking a short nap around 5:00 p.m., J.B. was rudely awaken by the sound of the closet door shaking. He stared in disbelief as the door began moving more violently and flew open. At the same time, the built-in desk and writing table opened up. This was the same table that the couple could not force open when they first arrived. After a minute or two, the violent shaking stopped. That weekend, they were also aware that several times after they left the room, and opened both port holes for air, they returned to find them closed and tightly latched. Instead of changing rooms, the couple decided to brave it out. They stayed without further incident.

WHEN THE CHEERING STOPPED

R.M. of Santa Barbara, California, recounted her night on board the ship with her boyfriend in Room M0127. At around 3:00 a.m., she was awakened by the odd sensation of the ship docking. She heard what sounded like the ship's lines being pulled in, and the **Queen Mary** beginning to move. She looked over at her boyfriend who was still asleep. As she got out of bed to look out the porthole, she heard the sound of people laughing and cheering, followed by a soft, but audible whisper of a man's voice saying, "Did you hear that?" R.M. became chilled, as she looked out the porthole into the clear, evening sky. The ship was safely docked, and there was no one outside cheering. The entire event lasted no more than ten seconds, and after that, there was only silence. R.M. had no idea what really happened. She couldn't get back to sleep very easily; however, her boyfriend slept through the entire event.

Children's party in 2nd Class Flamengo Room on the Main Deck

LITTLE GIRL <u>STILL</u> LOST

During one September, the authors were interviewed by a Japanese television station. We took them on a tour of the pool area, and shaft alley. While recounting the various paranormal tales that have circulated over the years, we concluded the interview in shaft alley, near watertight door Number 13. The crew had wrapped up our segment, and were preparing to interview another employee, when the interviewer, and the two of us heard the loud cries of a very young girl. Three times, the other-worldly youngster cried out, "Daddy, Daddy, Daddy!" Then there was silence. It wasn't a normal voice, it had an edge to it that seemed like it was coming from inside the very structure of the ship.

We felt an immediate sensation of cold, followed by an overwhelming sadness for the lost child. After a few seconds, it registered that what we heard was not the film crew, an employee, or other visitors, but a voice from beyond. In fact, we all remembered a segment of SIGHTINGS where psychic Peter James had gone into the boiler room with a camera crew, and recorded a child's voice on tape. That time, the child was distinctly heard yelling, "Mommy, Mommy, Mommy," three times. We hurried over to where the film crew was standing, not more than ten feet away, and asked them if they heard the child's voice. They had not.

We then ran through the maze of corridors, and checked the deck above to see if perhaps a group of children, or single child was wandering around without supervision. We found no one; no tour, no child without a parent, no employees. Except for the camera crew, interviewer, our guide from the ship and us, no one else was in the immediate area, or the deck above. We have no explanation for the event, other than the heavyhearted possibility that the ghostly child is trapped in another dimension, unable to find peace. She is aboard the **Queen Mary** searching for her parents, who allegedly were once passengers.

WHISPERS AT SIR WINSTON'S

Sir Winston's Restaurant is an elegant dining establishment on board the **Queen Mary**. It has an unrivaled view of Long Beach, and the cuisine is fabulous. It is also a place associated with a number of ghost stories including the Lady in White who seems to enjoy the piano bar. One episode occurred near the piano bar, where several employees were taking a break, and having a bite to eat. As they were talking, they were all hit with a blast of cold air that immediately caught their attention.

Since the area is self-contained, with no windows or doors opening to the outside, this was very unusual. As they rubbed their arms to warm up, they began hearing soft whispers of voices all around them, as if several people were sitting nearby. No one could make out what was being said, but for several seconds, the employees were enveloped in a blanket of cold air as voices from beyond were circulating through the room. Then, as quickly as the cold air had raced through the room, and the whispers

Guests relaxing in Lounge, circa 1938

began, it all stopped. No more cold, no more voices. Everything was back to "normal."

MAY I HELP YOU?

E.B., a Queen Mary employee recalled an experience she had during the Fall. As she was sitting in her office on the Sun Deck, conversing with a fellow worker, out of the corner of her eye, E.B. saw a woman enter the doorway to her department from the hallway. Initially, she assumed it was her boss, who usually says "hello," before entering her office. But this time there were no pleasantries exchanged. After a minute or so, E.B. called out. When no one responded, she assumed that it was a visitor or vendor who had entered the reception area for an appointment, instead of her boss. So, she called out again, "Hello, may I help you?" Still there was no reply.

Finally, she got up from her desk and walked into the reception area. There was no one there, so E.B. walked through the other offices. They were also deserted. From the moment that she saw the woman walk through the door, she was focused on that area, assuming that if it was a delivery person, she would see them leave. Although she saw a woman enter the office, she never saw anyone leave. According to E.B., "There is no way the woman could have left without me seeing them, unless she just vanished," which may have been exactly what happened!

NO PHOTOS PLEASE!

T.D.L. of California had a strange encounter during October, as follows. He went to visit his friend who works on the **Queen Mary**. They made reservations to spend the night and do some late night exploring, because of T.D.L's interest in the supernatural and the history of the ship. After checking in, the friend had a co-worker take them to the pool area after tour hours. Upon entering the area, it felt a dead calm, eerie, and silent. The men felt an intense loneliness, yet at the same time, as if they were being watched. They kept getting glimpses of people frolicking around the pool, and having fun. They could almost feel what it must have been like to be there in the late 1930s and 40s.

Guest's sketch of elderly female phantom swimmer

The nostalgic feelings began to overwhelm T.D.L. to the point of being a little frightened. He didn't want to leave without taking photographs, so he reluctantly climbed down a ladder and into the bottom of the drained pool. As soon as he reached the bottom of the pool, he couldn't stand the claustrophobic atmosphere. His friend joined him as her co-worker took photographs. He hated every minute down there, and after six shots, T.D.L. scurried back up the ladder with his friend in hot pursuit. T.D.L. had a picture taken of himself on the slide, and one in the dressing room area— eight photographs total.

After their little jaunt, T.D.L. and his friend retired to room M155. They were a little spooked after their pool excursion, so they kept the lights and television on all night—they might have slept an hour, at most. During the night, they kept hearing the sounds of someone opening the closet door, moving coat hangers around, then closing the door. This happened several times during the night, although the friends never saw the doors open once. Adding to the strange noises, their television managed to turn itself off at 4:30 a.m. A minute later, it came back on, as if someone invisible had done it. It was one strange night for the amateur ghost enthusiasts.

The next day, excited to see his photographs, T.D.L. rushed them to a one-hour photo developer. When he picked them up, all the photos on the roll turned out except for the shot around the pool. The negatives, were checked, and found to be all blank except for the one with T.D.L. on the slide. That negative had an image, but it would not come out. The photo shop could offer no explanation. T.D.L. plans to return and take more photographs. If they don't come out next time, he will take it as a hint that the phantom guests do not wish to have their picture taken!

LUCKY THIRTEEN

A.G. of Cypress, California was part of an October tour aboard the **Queen Mary**. The group of 13 individuals passed though most of the tour points without incident. Then, when the group reached the Boson's locker, their luck changed. As the tour guide was explaining the history of the ship and of this particular area, she looked and pointed toward the front. Just then, the room became icy cold. Everyone felt the chill, including the tour guide. Within seconds, a piece of metal fell to the floor, directly in front of the guide. Everyone jumped.

The guide proceeded to explain to the startled guests that things like this happened occasionally and not to worry. In fact, she said that a few days earlier, as she was taking a tour through the pool area, all the lights suddenly went out. When she went to call for help, the line went dead. Within a few minutes, the lights came on by themselves, and phone service was restored. The **Queen Mary** is a very spirited and unpredictable ship.

WEDDING BELL BLUES

Music publisher, S.H. of Los Angeles never had any experience with the paranormal and quite frankly, never thought she would. Because of her faith, she couldn't imagine such things. She didn't know if there was a history to the room she stayed in, or if anything abnormal had ever taken place there before. S.H. checked into the hotel around 4:45 p.m. on Friday night in October, and was assigned Room A162. The room was lovely and charming, and everything seemed in place. She hung up her clothes in the closet and arranged her personal things on the dresser near the porthole. The wedding took place in the chapel at 6:00 p.m., with a formal dinner and dancing following in the ballroom. Nothing out of the ordinary had happened during that time.

The reception had come to a close at midnight, but before they left, the bride told S.H. about what had happened earlier in the day. While in a room, the bride said that one of her ringbearers had been awakened from a nap and asked his mother who all the men were standing around the bed. Of course, his Mother had no answer, since no one else saw anything.

After listening to the story, S.H. and her boyfriend decided to go to the Observation Bar and listen to some music. After returning to their room, they turned on the television and got into bed. S.H. had left the curtains open over the portholes since she was a little jittery after hearing about ghosts on board the ship, and didn't want the room so dark that she could not see. The boyfriend fell asleep but S.H. lay awake all night. Shortly after her boyfriend fell asleep, S.H. heard a hollow clanging sound, like a pipe being banged on. Around 1:00 a.m., she was startled to hear sounds like someone moving the hangers in the clothes closet "like the little metal circles rolling across the wooden rod," a sound not unlike someone shuffling hangers to find something to wear, and loud enough to hear over the sound of the television. S.H. convinced herself that the noise was coming from the room next door.

The eerie noises didn't end with the shuffling hangars. After just dozing off around 3:30 a.m., she was abruptly awakened by the sound of someone trying to turn on the knob on the hurricane lamp hanging over her side of the bed. It went click, click, click, click, and was very loud, but S.H. was too afraid to look up—she just froze. She did not want to wake her boyfriend because he had his own experience with a spirit back in the Caribbean. However, S.H. did tell him about the strange occurrences when he woke up. He said S.H. was just being silly. However, when they were ready to leave the room to check out around 10:30 a.m., S.H. tried to turn on the lamp on the left side, but it wouldn't turn on. She turned and twisted the knob and it just kept clicking. She looked at her boyfriend, and told him that it was the exact same sound she had heard last night. The lamp finally came on by itself, and S.H. turned it back off. The couple left quickly. As they were leaving, S.H. realized that a hallway separated her closet from the next room, so the mystery hanger sounds could not have come from an adjacent room. How do you explain the mysterious events if you don't believe in ghosts?—S.H. couldn't.

THE MORGUE - A DEAD ISSUE

B.T. a former security guard, often encountered strange events while patrolling the area that once served as the morgue while the ship was at sea. many times the lights would suddenly go off and on when B.T. conducted an inspection. Sounds of doors opening and slamming shut were also frequently heard by B.T. and other guards. Many people have felt a cold rush of air engulf them while walking through this area, and although the doors are padlocked shut, they were often found open by unsuspecting guards. The most common feeling is that of being watched and followed, even though the guards patrol the area alone. The occasional sound of people whispering, or disembodied voices have also been heard, as a guard hurried through the area. Although it's a very lonely place to be at night, no one has every really felt alone there.

DOWSING FOR THE DEAD

A ghosthunter with dowsing equipment came aboard the **Queen Mary** in search of ghosts. After taking a series of readings, her was able to confirm three main charged areas aboard the ship where spirits were active. The first area was the side hallway between cabins B421 and B423. The second place was the staircase between the main deck and "A" deck, in the aft, starboard corner. The last spot was the 1st Class swimming pool, in the starboard corner. The man was certain there were many more paranormal "hot-spots" aboard, but during this particular walk-though, these three places were the most active. In fact, when the man was in the pool area, he felt something actually touch the back of his neck.

WHERE DO THE CHILDREN PLAY

L.S. of Placentia, California was on a tour of the ship when her tour group stopped in front of the nursery. The guide tried in vain to open the door, but couldn't, so the group moved on to the next exhibit as L.S. and her friend remained behind. As the tour group moved out of range, the two girls heard a clicking noise come from the door, as if someone were playing with the knob, trying to get in or out. As they watched for a

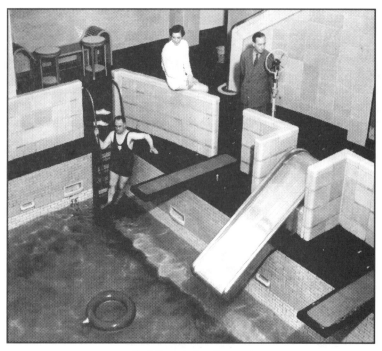

First Class swimming pool

moment, the noise stopped. L.S. and her friend finally caught up with the group, but several times during the remaining tour, L.S. felt someone tugging on her purse and skirt—it was not a group member. She also had the feeling of being followed. Ten minutes later, L.S. had the distinct sensation of someone tugging on her hair. "It was all very strange," L.S. said. Perhaps a child from the nursery became attached to L.S. and was following her for some unexplained reason.

THE COOK'S TOUR

A former cook in the employees' cafeteria had plenty to say about the ship's spirits. In her years of service, she has witnessed three plates fly through the air and crash to the floor when no one else was around. On other occasions, she came to work early and found the water pitchers reversed and resting on their tops in a neat alignment. Another time, while setting up a breakfast banquet at 3:30 a.m. she, and a group of employees were startled to hear what sounded like hundreds of dishes come crashing down in the kitchen. They all ran in expecting to see a huge mess, but there was nothing, no plates or anything out of place; yet everyone had heard the noise.

Service abourt ship

The cook tends to stay away from the exhibit hall, boiler room, and pool area because her fellow employees have reported so many strange events that have taken place there over the years. A little girl and a woman have been repeatedly sighted in the pool area, and small, wet footprints have been seen leading out of the pool toward the dressing room, even though the pool has been drained. Employees have repeatedly told the cook about seeing men in white or blue overalls working on equipment one minute, then vanishing in front of their eyes. Some of the doors to the exhibits will be found open even though they were securely locked. Apparitions, disembodied voices, and the constant unexplainable feelings of being watched or followed also frequently occur throughout the ship. "It's an eerie place to work," the cook stated. "I don't really mind sharing it with the spirits though, as long as they don't harm me. They haven't so far, and I don't think they will!"

FEELING DRAINED

A tour guide recalled her experience in the first class swimming pool. She was working as a tour guide in the pool area, and was waiting to get on the balcony for the tour group to come though the door. The guide was alone at the time and glanced over her right shoulder. She was startled to see an elderly woman wearing an old-fashioned, one-piece bathing suit that went up like a tank top, with a little bonnet or cap on her head. She had short curly hair sticking out from under the cap, but the guide immediately noticed that the mysterious elderly lady was visible to her in only in black and white.

The guide watched in amazement, unable to speak, as the figure was about to jump in the drained pool. The guide thought for a second that the elderly woman might be a tourist, and her first thought was to call security. In the moment it took to pick up the phone and look back at the woman, she had vanished. The guide quickly ran down the steps and searched the entire area, including the dressing room. The figure was nowhere to be seen, and there was no way for her to leave without being seen. The tour group came in, and although the guide gave the tour, her mind was on the strange elderly woman. Had she seen a ghost?

POOLING THEIR RESOURCES

Two tour guides were closing up the pool area after the last tour group had finished for the day. It was standard operating procedure, and they had done this numerous times without incident. This time, however, as they were standing on the edge of the pool platform, during a final inspection of the area, they heard a man clear his throat. After a few moments, the air became very cold, and the chain across the walkway began swinging back and forth, and twirling around repeatedly. Both tour guides quickly locked up and left the pool area as fast as they could. They went directly to the security office to report the strange event.

FEELING BLUE

On one occasion, a security guard on his way through shaft alley to make a final sweep of the area for straggling tourists, was coming back up the escalator. He was sure that he was the last person in the corridor, and he began turning off the lights and equipment, and blocking off the escalator route. As the guard walked into the south alley toward the two sets of escalators, he guard began ascending the open one. A few steps from the top, he had a feeling that someone was watching him from the bottom of the escalator. The guard took a quick look behind him. Sure enough, it was a man with dark hair, very pale skin, large dark eyes, and a nicely groomed black beard. He was wearing dirty, blue overalls. By now, the guard had reached the top of the escalator and the odd-looking man was half-way up.

The guard, thinking it was a maintenance person he had missed on his sweep of the area, stepped aside to let the man go by. In the split second that he turned away, and then back again, the man had disappeared! The guard remarked that he did not see the man appear or disappear, but he had somehow vanished in the Wink of an eye. The strange looking man never said a word, and didn't appear to be looking at the guard, but rather, straight ahead. The guard reported the incident, but never figured out where the man in the blue overalls had come from or gone to!

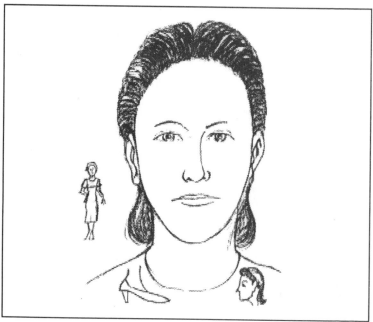

A guest's sketch of the phantom nurse

A BRUSH WITH DEATH

A couple arrived to spend a quiet, peaceful night aboard the *Queen Mary*. They were assigned room B462, and enjoyed a pleasant day on board the ship. As evening came, and it was time for bed, the husband was brushing his teeth, when he suddenly felt a constriction in his chest. Thinking it was the onset of a heart attack, he tried to speak to summon his wife. Within seconds, however, the tightening sensation passed, and he was able to breathe normally. Regaining his wits, the man realized that during a twenty second period, he had witnessed out of the corner of his eye, a young woman standing next to him in the bathroom. She appeared to be in her twenties, with brown hair, and was wearing a while camisole. By the time he was able to turn in the direction of the mystery lady, she had vanished! He wondered if brushing his tooth brushing had upset her by interfering with the young woman's own nightly other-worldly routine.

CLOSED DOORS WILL SOON BE OPENED

L.D., a business professional from Costa Mesa, California, was aboard the *Queen Mary* in December for a "Behind the Scenes" tour of the ship. There were around 20 people on the tour when the group passed the Third Class Nursery. L.D. and her sister noticed the door open slowly, then close, as they passed by the area,. The knob didn't turn, and the door didn't slam shut. As they stood their in silence, the same thing happened again. The door slowly opened without the knob turning, then quietly closed. It was as if two people exited the nursery, one after the other—the trouble was, you couldn't *see* anyone.

DON'T BANK ON IT

N.P., and banker from Florida, came to the ship to relax and get away from all the hustle and bustle of Miami's busy tourist environment. After checking into Room A123, a good night's sleep on a docked ship in Long Beach harbor seemed perfect for his needs—that is, until just before midnight. For approximately two hours, N.P. was kept awake by the sounds of several men talking outside his porthole. When he was first awakened by the conversations, he went over to the porthole and looked out. He was confused and more than a little frightened when he realized that he was facing Long Beach harbor. *No one* could be standing outside his room because there was no pier, deck, or other means of support for someone to be standing there. All he could do was try and tune out the voices, and conversations until they finally subsided. He heard about the haunted reputation of the ship, but really didn't think he believed in ghosts... that is, until now.

A HAIR RAISING EXPERIENCE

G.S. and his girlfriend Sara from Aptos, California, visited the *Queen Mary* during August and stayed in Room B511. During the night Sara was awakened at the stroke of midnight by someone stroking the back of her hair. Without turning to look, she asked G.S. to let her sleep and please stop playing with her hair. Finally, she turned over and realized that G.S. was still asleep. Sara grabbed and woke him up. She insisted that he had touched her hair several times. G.S. swore that he had been asleep the entire time and had no idea what Sara was talking about. A search of the newly remodeled room revealed nothing out of place, no sign of a visitor, and unfortunately no explanation for what had caused Sara's strange experience. The rest of the night was spent in the anticipation of another encounter. It never happened though. Apparently, once was enough.

First Class dining

SHATTERED SECRETS

J.K. and her sister came from Santee, California to spend the night aboard ship. J.K. while taking a tour of the **Queen Mary** by herself, wandered into the tourist lounge on the main deck at the stern of the ship around 9:00 p.m. While alone in the lounge, she suddenly felt extremely cold, and began rubbing her arms to keep warm. Within seconds J.K. heard several pieces of glass or china breaking as well as voices in heated conversation coming from inside the room. More than a little spooked, J.K. quickly glanced around; however no one had entered since she came in. The chills, strange noises, and stillness finally got to her. As she was about to leave, the voices stopped, and she noticed some broken plates in the right hand corner of the room. J.K. ran out of the doors and to the safety of her room.

THE (UN)LUCK OF THE IRISH

K.M.R of Winnetka, California related his story. K.R.M.'s sister-in-law Margaret, came over from Ireland for his wedding. She did not know the history of the **Queen Mary**. They had their reception in the Capstan room during the summer, and stayed for two nights. Around 12:45 a.m. Margaret went back to her state room, B304, to freshen up before going to the first class observation lounge to meet the wedding party. When she left, her mother and son were asleep.

The next morning they met up for breakfast and Margaret told them that her hairbrush and toothbrush were missing. She asked her mother and son if they had seen it, but they both said no. It was at that moment that K.M.R. told Margaret about the ship being haunted. About an hour later Margaret met up to take a tour of the boat and she told K.M.R. that she had found her brush in a bag under some clothes. When everyone checked out on Monday, Margaret still had not found her tooth brush. K.M.R. teased her that a well-groomed ghost was probably walking around with very clean teeth.

GHOSTLY GREETINGS

A.C. of Stanwood, Washington wrote us about her encounter aboard the ship in August. While standing by the grand staircase she heard ghostly voices of men and women talking although she saw no one around. She also picked up the scent of perfume and wine while hearing the sound of jewelry rattling, as if several people were walking up the stairs. She followed the sounds up the staircase and down a long hallway until she heard a scream come from in front of her. The hallway was completely empty, and A.C. left in a hurry.

Down in shaft alley, near water tight door Number 13, A.C. became chilled to the bone, and heard a loud banging noise coming from the area of the doorway. Out of the corner of her eye, she saw a ghostly child around eight-years-old, roughly three-feet-ten-inches tall, wearing 1940s clothing, looking in her direction. After a few seconds, the child vanished. Later on in the pool area, A.C. once again spotted the same young girl in the pool area standing in front of the long passageway near the lockers and shower peeking at A.C. before vanishing—a ghostly game of peek-a-boo!

The list of encounters appears endless, with stories as numerous as the ghosts who inhabit the ship. People from all walks of life have seen, heard, or felt something in certain areas of the ship—from Shaft Alley to the Bridge.

Ghosts rarely materialize; however, they do leave traces, if you are sensitive, or open enough to believe in the possibility of their existence. Hopefully, you will be one of the lucky few to be given a glimpse of their appearance, a touch indicating their presence, or a whisper of their name.

As a final thought, no one who has been involved in a paranormal event while on the ship has ever expressed a feeling of being threatened, or sensed that they would be harmed in any way. People have stated over and over that a healthy fear of the unknown has been present in most who have had an encounter; this is a natural emotion. In fact, the overall impression from crew and visitors alike, is that the experiences were refreshing, fun and exciting; and the ghosts aboard the ship appear to be friendly.

As one person said, "They are just doing their thing while we do ours. If we happen to enter their world, we should just say 'excuse me,' and move on."

Until then... *HAPPY HAUNTING !*

RECOMMENDED READING

Adams, Charles J. III
1982   Ghost Stories of Berks County, Exeter House Books, Reading, Pennsylvania.
1994   Pennsylvania Dutch Country Ghosts Legends and Lore, Exeter House Books, Reading, Pennsylvania.
1995   Berks The Bizarre, Exeter House Books, Reading, Pennsylvania
1996   New York City Ghost Stories: Chilling, True Encounters with the Supernatural in the World's Most Exciting, and Haunted City. Exeter House Books, Reading, Pennsylvania.
1997   Cape May Ghost Stories, Book 2. Exeter House Books, Reading, Pennsylvania.
1998   Philadelphia Ghost Stories, Exeter House Books, Pennsylvania.
1999   Bucks County Ghost Stories, Exeter House Books, Reading, Pennsylvania

Adams, Charles J. III, and Gary Lee Clothier
1988,   Ghost Stories of Berks County, Book 3. Exeter House Books, Reading, Pennsylvania

Adams, Charles J. III, and David J. Seibold
1993   Ghost Stories of the Lehigh Valley. Exeter House Books, Reading, Pennsylvania
1995   Pocono Ghosts, Legends, and Lore, Book Two. Exeter House Books, Reading, Pennsylvania

Anderson, Jean
1973   The Haunting of America. Houghton Mifflin Company, Boston

Balliett, Blue
1984   The Ghosts of Nantucket: 23 True Accounts, Down East Books, Camden, Maine.

Beckett, John
1991   World's Wierdest "True" Ghost Stories. Sterling Publishing Company, Inc., New York.

Bielski, Ursula
1997   Chicago Haunts: Ghostly Lore of the Windy City. Lake Claremont Press, Chicago, Illinois.

Bingham, Joan, and Dolores Riccio
1991   More Haunted Houses. Pocket Books, N.Y.

Blackman, W. Haden,
1998   The Field Guide to North American Hauntings. Three Rivers Press, New York.

Blue & Gray Magazine
1996   Guide to Haunted Places of the Civil War. Blue & Gray Enterprises, Inc. Columbus, Ohio.

Boyer, Dennis
1998   Northern Frights. Prairie Oak Press, Madison, Wisconsin

Bradley, Nancy
1998   The Incredible World of Gold Rush Ghosts, Morris Publishing, Kearney, Nebraska

Bradley, Nancy and Vincent Gaddis
1990   Gold Rush Ghosts, Borderland Sciences, Garberville, California

Buckland, Raymond (editor)
1996   Guide to Haunted Places of the Civil War. Blue & Gray Enterprises, Inc.
          Columbus, Ohio.
1991   Ghosts, Hauntings and Possessions: The Best of Hans Holzer Book Lllewellyn
          Publications, St. Paul, Minnesota.

Burnett, Claudine
1996   Haunted Long Beach. Historical Society of Long Beach. Long Beach, California.

Cahill, Robert Ellis
1963   New England's Ghostly Haunts. Chandler-Smith Publishing House, Inc.
1992   Haunted Happenings. Old Saltbox Publishing House, Inc. Salem, Massachusetts.
1998   Lighthouse Mysteries of the North Atlantic. Old Saltbox Publishing House,
          Inc. Salem, Massachusetts.

Cartmell, Connie Cartmell
1996   Ghosts of Marietta, The River Press, Marietta, Ohio

Clearfield, Dylan
1997   Chicagoland Ghosts, Thunder Bay Press, Grand Rapids, Michigan.

Clifton, Charles
1993   Ghost Stories of Cripple Creek, Little London Press, Colorado Springs, Colorado.

Cohen, Daniel
1977   Real Ghosts. Pocket Books, New York.
1984   The Encyclopedia of Ghosts. Dodd, Mead and Co. N.Y.

Coleman, loren
1983   Mysterious America. Faber & Faber Winchester, Massachusetts.

Courtaway, Robbi
1999   Spirits of Saint Louis, Virginia Publishing Company, St. Louis, Missouri

Crites, Susan
1997   Lively Ghosts Along The Potomac. Butternut Publication, Martinsburg,
          West Virginia.

DeBolt, Margaret Wayt
1984   Savannah Specters and Other Strange Tales. The Donning Company
          Publishers, Norfolk, Virginia Beach.

Discover Travel Adventures
1990   Haunted Holidays. Discovery Communications, Inc. Insight Guides, Langenscheidt Publishers, Inc., Maspeth, New York.

Elizabeth, Norma and Bruce Roberts
1999   Lighthouse Ghosts, Crane Hill Publishers, Birmingham, Alabama

Duffey, Barbara
1996   Angels and Apparitions: True Ghost Stories from the South. Elysian Publishing Company, Eatonton, Georgia.

Floyd, Blanche W.
1999   Tales Along the King's Highway of South Carolina. Bandit Books, Winston-Salem, North Carolina.

Forman, Joan
1978   The Haunted South. Jarrold Publications, Norwich, Great Britain.

Franklin, Dixie
1997   Haunts of the Upper Great Lakes, Thunder Bay Press, Michigan

Garcez, Antonio
1994   Adobe Angels: The Ghosts of Albuquerque. Red Rabbit Press, Truth or Consequences, New Mexico.
1995   Adobe Angels: The Ghosts of Santa Fe and Taos. Red Rabbit Press, Truth or Consequences, New Mexico.
1996   Adobe Angels: The Ghosts of Las Cruces & Southern New Mexico. Red Rabbit Press, Truth or Consequences, New Mexico.
1998   Adobe Angels: Arizona Ghost Stories. Red Rabbit Press, Truth or Consequences, New Mexico.

Grant, Glen
1996,   Obake Files, Mutual Publishing, Honolulu, Hawaii.

Gruber, Suzanne and Bob Wasel
1998   Haunts of the Cashtown Inn. Bob Wasel, Pennsylvania.

Guiley, Rosemary
1992   The Encyclopedia of Ghosts and Spirits. Facts on File, New York

Hauck, Dennis William
1996   The National Directory Haunted Places: Ghostly Abodes, Sacred Sites, UFO landings, and Other Supernatural Locations. Penguin Books, New York.

Hein, Ruth D. and Vicky Hinsenbrock
1996   Ghostly Tales of Iowa, Iowa State University Press, Ames.

Heitz, Lisa Hefner
1997   Haunted Kansas, University Press of Kansas, Lawrence.

Henson, Michael Paul
1996   More Kentucky Ghost Stories. The Overmountain Press, Johnson City, Tennessee.

Hoffman, Elizabeth P.
1992   Haunted Places in the Delaware Valley. Camino Books, Philadelphia

Holzer, Hans
1968   Ghosts of the Golden West. The Bobbs-Merrill Co. N.Y./also Ace Books.
1971   The Phantoms of Dixie, Bobbs-Merrill Company, Indiana
1974   Haunted Hollywood. The Bobbs-Merril Co. N.Y.
1988   Great American Short Stories. Barners & Noble Books, Inc. New York.
1990   Great American Ghost Stories. Dorset Press, New York
1992   Ghosts of Old Europe. Dorset Press, New York.
1992   Haunted House Album. Dorset Press, New York.
1993   America's Restless Ghosts. Longmeadow Press, Stamford, Connecticuit.
1995   Where The Ghosts Are: The Ultimate Guide To Haunted Houses. A Citadel Press Book, New York.
1997   Ghosts: True Encounters with the World Beyond. Haunted Places, Haunted Houses, Haunted People. Black Dog and Leventhal Publishers, New York, New York.

Hubbard, Sylvia Booth
1992   Ghosts! Personal Accounts of Modern Mississippi Hauntings, QRP Books, Brandon, Mississippi

Huntsinger, Elizabeth Robertson
1995   Ghosts of Georgetown (1995), John F. Blair, North Carolina.

Jacobson, Laurie, and Marc. Wanamaker
1994   Hollywood Haunted. A Ghostly Tour of Filmland. Angel City Press, Santa Monica.
1999   Hollywood Haunted (Revised Edition), Angel City Press, Santa Monica, California

Jarvis, Sharon
1992   Dead Zones. Warner Books, Inc. New York.

Jeffrey, Adi-Kent Thomas
1971   Ghosts in the Valley: Delaware Valley, Hampton Publishing, Hampton, Pennsylvania

Kaczmarek, Dale
1999   National Register of Haunted Locations. Ghost Research Society, P.O. Box 205, Oak Lawn, Illinois

Kuclo, Marion
1996   Michigan Haunts and Hauntings. Thunder Bay Press, Lansing, Michigan.

Kutz, Jack
1996   Mysteries and Miracles of California. Rhombus Publishing Company, Corrales, New Mexico.

L'Aloge, Bob
1991   Ghosts and Mysteries of the, Yucca Tree Press, Las Cruces, New Mexico

Lamb, John J.
1999   San Diego Specters. Sunbelt Publications, San Diego, California.

Linn, Denise
1995   Sacred Space: Clearing and Enhancing the Energy of Your Home. Ballantine
        Books, New York.

Longo, Jim
1993   Ghosts Along the Mississippi, Haunted Odyssey II. Ste. Anne's Press,
        St. Louis, Missouri.

MacDonald, Margaret Read
1995   Ghost Stories from the Pacific Northwest. August House Publishers, Inc.
        Little Rock, Arkansas.

Marimen, Mark
1997   Haunted Indiana. Thunder Bay Press, Lansing, Michigan.

Marinacci, Mike
1988   Mysterious California. Panpipes Press. Los Angeles.

Martin, Maryjoy
1985   Twilight Dwellers: The Ghosts, Ghouls and Goblins of Colorado.
        Pruett Publishing, Boulder Colorado.

May, Alan M.
1990   The Legend of Kate Morgan , Elk Publishing, San Marcos, California.

May, Antoinette
1977   Haunted Houses and Wandering Ghosts of California. San Francisco
        Examiner Special Projects, San Francisco.
1993   Haunted Houses of California. Wide World Publishing/retra. San Carlos, California.

MacDonald, Margaret Read
1995   Ghost Stories From The Pacific Northwest. American Folklore Series, August
        House Publishers, Inc. Little Rock, Arkansas.

McNeil, W.K.
1985   Ghost Stories from the American South. August House, Little Rock, Arkansas.

Mead, Robin
1995   Haunted Hotels: A Guide to American and Canadian Inns and Their Ghosts.
        Rutledge Hill Press, Nashville, Tennessee.

Michaels, Susan
1996   Sightings: Beyond Imagination Lies The Truth. A Fireside Book published by
        Simon & Schuster, New York.

Morrison, Nannette
1994   Echoes of Valor. Bookwrights of Charlottesville. Charlottesville, Virginia.
1996   A Thundering Silence. Bookwrights of Charlottesville. Charlattesville, Virginia.

Munn, Debra
1994   Big Sky Ghosts. Pruett Publishing, Boulder, Colorado.

Murray, Earl
1988   Ghosts of the Old West, Barnes & Noble Books, New York.

Myers, Arthur
1986   The Ghostly Register. Contemporary Books. Chicago.
1990   The Ghostly Gazetteer: America's Most Fascinating Haunted Landmark.
          Con temporary Books. Chicago.
1993   A Ghosthunter's Guide To Haunted Landmarks, Parks, Churches, and Other
          Public Places. Contemporary Books, Chicago.

Nadler, Holly Mascott
1994   Haunted Island, Down East Books, Camden, Maine.

Nesbitt, Mark
1991   Ghosts of Gettysburg, Spirits, Apparitions and Haunted Places of the
          Battlefield. Thomas Publicatians, Gettysburg, Pennsylvania.
1992   More Ghosts of Gettysburg, Spirits, Apparitions and Haunted Places of the
          Battlefield. Thomas Publications, Gettysburg, Pennsylvania.
1995   Ghosts of Gettysburg III, Spirits, Apparitions and Haunted Places of the
          Battlefield. Thomas Publications, Gettysburg, Pennsylvania.
1998   Ghosts of Gettysburg IV, Spirits, Apparitions and Haunted Places of the
          Battlefield. Thomas Publications, Gettysburg, Pennsylvania.

Norman, Michael, and Beth Scott
1994   Haunted America. A Tom Doherty Asssociates Book. New York.
1995   Historic Haunted Ameirca. A Tom Doherty Associates Book, New York.

Norman, Diana
1977   The Stately Ghosts of England. Dorset Press. N.Y.

Oester, Dave, and Sharon Gill
1995   Twilight Visitors: Ghost Tales, Volume One. StarWest Images, St. Helens, Oregon.
1996   The Haunted Reality. StarWest Images, St. Helens, Oregon.

Okonowicz, Ed
1994   Spirits Between the Bays: Vol. I, Pulling Back the Curtain. Myst and Lace
          Publishers, Inc., 1386 Fair Hill Lane, Elkton, Maryland.
1995   Spirits Between the Bays: Vol. II, Opening the Door. Myst and Lace
          Publishers, Inc., 1386 Fair Hill Lane, Elkton, Maryland.
1995   Spirits Between the Bays: Vol. III, Welcome Inn. Myst and Lace
          Publishers, Inc., 1386 Fair Hill Lane, Elkton, Maryland.
1996   Spirits Between the Bays: Vol. IV, In the Vestibule. Myst and Lace Publishers,
          Inc., 1386 Fair Hill Lane, Elkton, Maryland.

Okonowicz, Ed
1996   Possessed Possessions: Haunted Antiques, Furniture, and Collectibles. Myst and Lace Publishers, Inc., 1386 Fair Hill Lane, Elkton, Maryland.
1997   Spirits Between the Bays: Vol. V, Spirits Between the Bays. Myst and Lace Publishers, Inc., 1386 Fair Hill Lane, Elkton, Maryland.
1998   Crying in the Kitchen: Stories of Ghosts that Roam the Water. Vol. VI, Myst and Lace Publishers, Inc., 1386 Fair Hill Lane, Elkton, Maryland.
1999   Up the Back Stairway, Spirits Between the Bays Series, Myst and Lace Publishers, Inc., 1386 Fair Hill Lane, Elkton, Maryland.

Ogden, Tom
1999   The Complete Idiot's Guide to Ghosts and Hauntings, Alpha Books, Indianapolis, Indiana.

Pitkin, David J.
1998   Saratoga County Ghosts, Aurora Publications, Ballston Spa, New York.

Price, Edwin Charles
1995   Haunted Tennessee. The Overmountain Press, Johnson City, Tennessee.

Randles, Jenny, and Peter Hough
1993   The Afterlife.: An Investigation Into the Mysteries of Life After Death. Berkley Books, N.Y.

Readers Digest
1993   Quest For The Unknown: Ghosts and Hauntings. The Readers Digest Association, Inc. Pleasantville, New York.

Reinstedt, Randall
1977   Ghostly Tales and Mysterious Happennings of Old Monterey. Ghost Town Publications, Carmel, California.
1980   Incredible Ghosts of Old Monterey's Hotel Del Monte. Ghost Town Publications, Carmel, California.

Rhyne, Nancy
1989   Coastal Ghosts. Sandlapper Publishing, Inc. Orangeburg, South Carolina.

Roberts, Andy
1992   Ghosts and Legends of Yorkshire. Jarrold Press, Norwich, England

Roberts, Bruce, and Nancy
1988   Prologue. In, The Haunted South: Where Ghosts Still Roam by Nancy Roberts. University of South Carolina Press, Columbia, South Carolina.

Roberts, Nancy
1967   North Carolina Ghosts and Legends. University of South Carolina Press, Columbia, South Carolina.
1967   Ghosts of the Carolinas. University of South Carolina Press, Columbia, South Carolina.

Roberts, Nancy
1974   America's Most Haunted Places. Sandlapper Publishing Company,
        Orangeburg, South Carolina.
1979   Southern Ghosts. Sandlapper Publishing Company, Orangeburg, South Carolina.
1983   South Carolina Ghosts: From the Coast to the Mountains. University of South
        Carolina Press, Columbia, South Carolina.
1984   Ghosts and Specters of the Old South, Sandlapper Publishing Company,
        South Carolina
1988   The Haunted South: Where Ghosts Still Roam. University of South Carolina
        Press, Columbia, South Carolina.
1988   Ghosts of the Southern Mountains and Appalachia. University of South
        Carolina Press, Columbia, South Carolina.
1992   Ghosts of the Carolinas, University of South Carolina Press, Columbia,
        South Carolina.
1992   This Haunted Southland. University of South Carolina Press, Columbia,
        South Carolina.
1993   Ghosts of the Southern Mountains and Appalachia. University of South
        Carolina Press, Columbia, South Carolina.
1995   Haunted Houses: Chilling Tales from Nineteen American Homes. The Globe
        Pequot Press, Old Saybrook, Connecticut.
1997   Georgia Ghosts. John F. Blair, Publisher. Winston-Salem, North Carolina
1998   Haunted Houses: Chilling Tales From 24 American Homes, The Globe Pequot
        Press, Old Saybrook, Connecticut.

Robinson, Charles Turek
1994   The New England Ghost Files, An Authentic Compendium of Frightening
        Phantoms. Covered Bridge Press, Maryland.

Robson, Ellen and Diane Halicki
1999   Haunted Highway, The Spirits of Route 66 (1999). Golden West Publishers,
        Phoenix, Arizona.

Roth, David
1996   Preface. In, Blue & Gray Magazine, Guide to Haunted Places of the Civil War.
        Blue & Gray Enterprises, Inc. Columbus, Ohio.

Ruth, Kent
1963   Landmarks of the West: A Guide to Historic Sites. University of Nebraska
        Press, Lincoln

Schulte, Carol Olivieri
1989   Ghosts on the Coast of Maine. Down East Books, Camden, Maine.

Schwalm, Maurice
1999   Mo-Kan Ghosts, Belfry Books, Laceyville, Pennsylvania.

Scott, Beth, and Michael Norman
1980   Haunted Wisconsin. Heartland Press, Minocqua, Wisconsin.
1987   Haunted Heartland. Warner Books. New York.

Segal, Eric
1975   Alexandria Ghosts. The Alexandria Bicentennial Youth Commission.

Seibold, David J., and Charles J. Adams III
1988   Cape May Ghost Stories. Exeter House Books, Reading, Pennsylvania.
1990   Ghost Stories of the Delaware Coast. Exeter House Books, Reading, Pennsylvania.
1991   Pocono Ghosts, Legends, and Lore. Exeter House Books, Reading, Pennsylvania.
1995   Pocono Ghosts, Legends, and Lore, Book Two. Exeter House Books, Reading, Pennsylvania.

Senate, Richard L.
1986   Ghosts of Southern California. Pathfinder Publishing. Ventura.
1985   Ghosts of the Haunted Coast. Pathfinder Publishing. Ventura.
1994   The Haunted Southland. Charon Press, Ventura, California.
1998   Ghost Stalker's Guide to Haunted California. Charon Press, Ventura, California.
1998   Ghosts of the Ojai: California's Most Haunted Valley. Charon Press,
          Ventura, California.

Sharp, Eleyne Austen
1996   Haunted Newport, Austen Sharp Publishing, P.O. Box 12, Newport, Rhode
Island.
1999   Haunted Newport. Austen Sharp, Newport Rhode Island.

Smoller, Daena
1988   The Official ISPR Self-Guided Ghost Expedition of New Orleans. ISPR,
          P.O. Box 291159, Los Angeles, California.

Spencer, John and Tony Wells
1994   Ghost Watching: The Ghosthunter Handbook. Virgin Publishing Ltd., London.

Steiger, Brad
1995   The Awful Thing in the Attic. Glade Press, Inc. St. Paul, Minnesota.

Steiger, Sherri Hansen, and Brad Steiger
1990   Hollywood and the Supernatural. St. Martin's Press.

Stonehouse, Frederick
1997   Haunted Lakes: Great Lakes Ghost Stories, Superstitions, and Sea Serpents.
          Lake Superior Port Cities, Inc., Duluth, Minnesota.

Svehla, Gary J. and Susan (editors)
1996   Cinematic Hauntings. Midnight Marquee Press, Inc., Baltimore, Maryland.

Swetnam, George
1998   Devils, Ghosts & Witches, McDonald/Sward, Greensburg, Pennsylvania.

Taylor, L.B. Jr.
1983   The Ghosts of Williamsburg. 108 Elizabeth Meriwether, Williamsburg, Virginia.
1985   The Ghosts of Richmond. 108 Elizabeth Meriwether, Williamsburg, Virginia.
1990   The Ghosts of Tidewater. 108 Elizabeth Meriwether, Williamsburg, Virginia.

Taylor, L.B. Jr.
1991   The Ghosts of Fredericksburg. 108 Elizabeth Meriwether, Williamsburg, Virginia.
1992   The Ghosts of Charlottesville and Lynchburg. 108 Elizabeth Meriwether, Williamsburg, Virginia.
1993   The Ghosts of Virginia. 108 Elizabeth Meriwether, Williamsburg, Virginia.
1994   The Ghosts of Virginia, Volume II. 108 Elizabeth Meriwether, Williamsburg, Virginia.
1996   The Ghosts of Virginia, Volume III. 108 Elizabeth Meriwether, Williamsburg, Virginia.
1998   The Ghosts of Virginia, Volume IV. 108 Elizabeth Meriwether, Williamsburg, Virginia.
1999   The Ghosts of Williamsburg, Volume II. 108 Elizabeth Meriwether, Williamsburg, Virginia.

Taylor, Troy
1995   Haunted Decatur. Whitechapel Productions Press, 515 East Third Street, Alton, Illinois.
1996   More Haunted Decatur. Whitechapel Productions Press, 515 East Third Street, Alton, Illinois.
1996   Ghosts of Millikin: The History of Millikin University. Haunted Decatur Book 3. Whitechapel Productions Press, 515 East Third Street, Alton, Illinois.
1997   Where the Dead Walk: The Haunted History of Greenwood Cemetery. Haunted Decatur Book 4. Whitechapel Productions Press, 515 East Third Street, Alton, Illinois.
1997   Ghosts of Springfield, The Haunted History of Abraham Lincoln and the Spirits of the Prairie Capital. Ghosts of the Prairie Series Book One. Whitechapel Productions Press, 515 East Third Street, Alton, Illinois.
1997   Dark Harvest, The Compleat Haunted Decatur. Haunted Decatur Series. Whitechapel Productions Press, 515 East Third Street, Alton, Illinois.
1998   The Ghost Hunter's Handbook: The Essential How-to Guide for Investigating Ghosts and the Paranormal. Whitechapel Productions Press, 515 East Third Street, Alton, Illinois.
1998   Ghosts of Little Egypt. Whitechapel Productions Press, 515 East Third Street, Alton, Illinois.
1999   Spirits of the Civil War: A Guide to the Ghost and Hauntings of America's Bloodiest Conflict. Whitechapel Productions Press, 515 East Third Street, Alton, Illinois.
1999   Haunted Illinois: Ghosts and Hauntings from Egypt to the Windy City. Whitechapel Productions Press, 515 East Third Street, Alton, Illinois.

Viviano, Christy
1992   Haunted Louisiana. Tree House Press, Metairie, Louisiana.

Ward, Frank
1998   Close Behind Thee (1998), Whitechapel Productions, Forsyth, Illinois.

Warren, Ed and Lorraine, and Robert David Chase
1991   Ghost Hunters. St. Martin's Paperbacks, N.Y.
1992   Graveyard: True Tales from and Old New England Cemetery. St. Martin's Paperbacks, N.Y.

Warren, Joshua P.
1996   Haunted Asheville. Shadowbox Publications. Asheville, North Carolina.

Watson, Daryl
1995   Ghosts of Galena. Galena/Jo Daviess County Historic Society, Galena. Illinois.

Williams, Docia Schultz
1995   Ghosts Along The Texas Coast. Republic of Texas Press, Plano, Texas.
1996   Phantoms of the Plains: Tales of West Texas Ghosts. Republic of Texas Press, Plano, Texas.
1997   When Darkness Falls: Tales of San Antonio Ghosts and Hauntings. Republic of Texas Press, Plano, Texas.
1998   Best Tales of Texas Ghosts. Republic of Texas Press, Plano, Texas.

Williams, Docia Schultz, and Reneta Byrne
1993   Spirits of San Antonio and South Texas. Repubiic of Texas Press, Plano, Texas.

Windham, Kathryn Tucker
1971   Jeffrey Introduces 13 More Southern Ghosts. The University of Alabama Press, Tuscaloosa.
1973   13 Georgia Ghosts and Jeffrey. The University of Alabama Press, Tuscaloosa.
1974   13 Mississippi Ghosts and Jeffrey. The University of Alabama Press, Tuscaloosa.
1977   13 Tennessee Ghosts and Jeffrey. The University of Alabama Press, Tuscaloosa.
1982   Jeffrey's Latest 13: More Alabama Ghosts. The University of Alabama Press, Tuscaloosa.

Windham, Kathryn Tucker, and Margaret Gillis Figh
1969   13 Alabama Ghosts and Jeffrey. The University of Alabama Press, Tuscaloosa.

Winer, Richard, and Nancy Osborn
1979   Haunted Houses. Bantam Books. N.Y.

Wlodarski, Robert J., and Anne P. Wlodarski
1996   Haunted Catalina: A History of the Island and Guide to Paranormal Activity. G-Host Publishing, West Hills, California.
1996   The Haunted Alamo: A History ofthe Mission and Guide to Paranormal Activity. G-Host Publishing, West Hills, California.
1997   The Haunted Whaley House. A History and Guide to the Most Haunted House in America. G-Host Publishing, West Hills, California.
1999   Spirits of the Alamo: A History of the Mission and its Hauntings. Republic of Texas Press, Wordware Publishing, Plano, Texas.
2000   Southern Fried Spirits: A Guide to Haunted Restaurants, Taverns and Inns Republic of Texas Press, Wordware Publishing, Plano, Texas.
2000   Dinner and Spirits: A Guide to America's Most Haunted Restaurants, Taverns, and Inns. iUniverse Publishing, New York, New York.
2000   The Haunted Queen Mary, Long Beach, California. G-Host Publishing, West Hills, California.

Wlodarski, Robert J., Anne Nathan-Wlodarski, and Michael J. Kouri
1998   Haunted Alcatraz: A History of La isla de los Alcatraces and Guide to Paranormal Activity. G-Host Publishing, West Hills, California.

Wlodarski, Robert J., Anne Nathan-Wlodarski, and Richard Senate
1995   A Guide To the Haunted Queen Mary: Ghostly Apparitions, Psychic Phenomena and Paranormal Activity. G-Host Publishing, West Hills, California

Wood, Ted
1997   Ghosts of the Southwest, Walker and Company, New York.
1999   Ghosts of the West Coast. Walker and Company, New York

Woodyard, Chris
1991   Haunted Ohio. Kestral Publications, 1811 Stonewood Drive, Beavercreek, Ohio.
1992   Haunted Ohio II. Kestral Publications, 1811 Stonewood Drive, Beavercreek, Ohio.
1994   Haunted Ohio III: Still More Ghostly Tales from the Buckeye State. Kestral Publications, 1811 Stonewood Drive, Beavercreek, Ohio.
1997   Haunted Ohio IV: Restless Spirits. Kestral Publications, 1811 Stonewood Drive, Beavercreek, Ohio.

Yeates, Geoff
1994   Cambridge College Ghosts. Jarrold Publishing, Norwich, Great Britain.

Young, Richard Dockrey and Judy Dockrey Young
1991   Ghost Stories from the American Southwest (1991), August House, Little Rock, Arkansas.

Zepke, Terrance
1999   Ghosts of the Carolina Coasts. Pineapple Press, Inc. Sarasota, Florida.

TO ORDER BOOKS ON GHOSTS CONTACT:

Troy Taylor - *Whitechapel Productions Press & Riverboat Molly's* - A History & Hauntings Book Co. - Home of the American Ghost Society, 515 East Third Street - Alton, Illinois 62002, (618) 465-1086 / Fax: (618) 465-1085 - Toll Free Ordering Number: 1-888-GHOSTLY - E-mail: ttaylor@prairieghosts.com - "Ghosts of the Prairie" - http://www.prairieghosts.com

Chris Woodyard - *Invisible Ink* - Books on Ghosts & Hauntings - 1811 Stonewood Drive, Dayton, Ohio 45432 - 1-800-31-GHOST - Fax: 937-320-1832 - E-mail: invisible@aol.com

WHAT TO DO IF YOU SEE A GHOST ON THE QUEEN MARY

1. Don't panic, sit back and enjoy the phenomenon and try to notice every detail you can.

2. After the event, write down exactly what you saw in as much detail as possible. Remember if there were any particular smells, sensations such as cold spots, gusts of air, or feelings of nausea; music playing or other audible sounds, voices or conversations in the background, or feelings of being watched or touched, etc.

3. Try and sketch what you saw: what the image was wearing, include the style of clothing, shoes, glasses, hats, etc., anything which may give an indication of a particular time period or era.

4. Draw a diagram or map of where the apparition was seen and where you were when the event took place. Note wallpaper, furnishings, types of windows, flooring, or other features in relation to the sighting.

5. Note what time of the day the event took place as well as weather conditions and temperature, if possible.

6. Record general information regarding how the event made you feel (happy, sad, depressed, frightened).

7. Note any unusual circumstances surrounding the event including; storms, power outages, other people working in the area, etc.).

8. Note other people present; include any children or animals who might have witnessed the event or may have been affected.

9. Attempt to investigate the experience further including who the ghost might have been: Attempt to rule out any explainable causes for the occurrence and try to research the area in more detail.

10. If you are able to summon the courage, talk to the spirit in a sincere manner and tell it to pass on to the next realm by looking for and following the white light—prayers to release a trapped spirit oftentimes yield positive results.

TIPS FOR RELEASING A TROUBLESOME SPIRIT

This information was taken from Claudine Burnett's book, **Haunted Long Beach** (1996) which was extracted from Denise Linn in her book entitled **Sacred Space** (1995). According to Linn, tips for dealing with sometimes unwanted ghosts include:

1. Clean the room or rooms in which you have had the unearthly encounters.

2. Burn a mixture of sea salt or Epsom salts and alcohol in the room— [white sage is also used].

3. Take some salt and sprinkle an entire circle around the area of the sighting, leaving a small opening in the circle by a window or a door for the spirit to exit through. Make sure the door or window is open— [sprinkling salt in the four interior or exterior corners of the house or structure can also be performed].

4. Burn a seven-day candle close to where you've seen the ghost.

5. Tell the ghost out loud, three times, "You are now free to go to the Light!" These words must be spoken with authority and certainty.

6. Strike a gong or ring a bell and tell the spirit again, three times, to go to the Light immediately.

7. Ask the help of others from the "other side" to guide your ghost to the next realm.

8. Leave the candle constantly burning for the seven days as a focal point for the helpers from the "other side" to come and continue to offer help to the restless spirit if needed.

According to Claudine Burnett's friend Holly, who grew up in Vietnam, a Vietnamese friend, ghosts are very much a part of the woman's culture; by burning incense or offering a bowl of fruit to any lingering entity that may reside in a new house they might move into seems to keep them away (Burnett (1996:77). A number of other techniques includes prayers, blessings, incense, holy water, salt, sage, and exorcisms in drastic situations. There are also those individuals and persons who don't mind sharing their space with ghosts, seemingly content to tolerate the noises, visitations, and pranks. Finally, there are those who seem to prefer the companionship of the dead to that of the living, and while having someone invisible to talk to and listen to them at any time of the day or night, they do not have to pay for their upkeep.

THE GHOST HUNTERS' KIT

Permission to use the following information was granted by Richard Senate. Check out his web site (www.phantoms.com/ghost.htm or www.ghost-stalkers.com. In the investigations of haunted sites, Senate has put together a collection of tools he has have found useful.

1. 35mm camera loaded with XXX black and white film. A red gel should be placed over the flash unit. This causes the ASA to push into the infrared Spec trum [do not know why it works but using this configuration I have managed to take photographs of ghosts]. A stereo camera is also useful. Take along at least two cameras—one loaded with high speed film for low light and the other with XXX Film.

2. Tape Recorder with a microphone that is external. Use music quality tape and Always use Brand new tape! Never use the Chromium Oxide tape as some times a voice might double record. Use in walk-though of haunted sites. When you are in a haunted place you may hear nothing! It is only when the tape is played back to spirit voices come out. They have a harsh, whispered quality and they only say one or two words, less than a sentence. This is called EVP for Electronic Voice Phenomena. Take along two tape recorders. One just as a back-up with regular tape and a built in mike.

3. A good flash light—but even the best can fail when you enter a haunted site— it seems that ghosts can manipulate electronic units. Sometimes a good kerosene lantern is better or a good old candle and match.

4. Notebook of paper and a pen is one of the best tools to save data. Write down all that you see and feel and record the times when it happened —Keep a journal of your overnight ghost stake-out. Paper is also useful for drawing floor-plans of the haunted site and sketching a likeness of any ghosts you happen to see.

5. A Compass. This small thing can be very helpful in finding your way around county back roads and in mapping out a site. Also, I have found that a compass needle may act strangely in haunted places.

6. A good EM Detector (Or Gauss Meter) is very good tool. Ghosts are found in electro- magnetic fields. We still do not know why, but there is some interesting new research being done on this phenomena.

7. Thermometers are always of help in any ghost hunt. Electronic ones are excellent but ghosts can manipulate them. Any change in the surrounding environment can indicate the presence of a phantom. For countless centuries people have felt an icy cold in haunted places. Some cold spots have a six degree difference in temperature and in some of the literature twenty degrees are recorded in haunted

rooms (I haven't encountered that much of a temperature difference yet!)

8. Silver Cross and a small bottle of HOLY WATER. (One can never be too careful you know-like chicken soup it can't hurt). Over the years silver has been liked to psychic events and I have noticed that women who wear a lot of silver jewelry seem to have more ghostly sightings—Why?I don't know.

9. Dowsing Rods have been used for centuries to find water. But, strange as it sounds they can be used to find areas of psychic disturbances. They seem to react in places of murder and death, places where ghosts and poltergeists infest. Almost anyone can use dowsing rods and find lost items, and places where ghosts are found—but be sure you are not just finding buried water pipes! A little practice and you will discover how useful dowsing rods can be! If you wish to understand more of how ghost hunters seek answers to the riddle of a haunted house read my book **The Haunted Southland**. If you should snap a picture of a ghost or pick up a phantom voice on tape please let me know and I can help you determine if it is real or accidental.

[DOCUMENTING YOUR OWN EXPERIENCES ABOARD THE QUEEN MARY]

NAME_____.

ADDRESS_____.

CITY_____STATE_____.

ZIP CODE_____-_____.

PHONE (HOME:_____.   OTHER NUMBER: _____.

BIRTH DATE _____.   OCCUPATION_____.

MARRIED_____   SINGLE_____   NO. OF CHILDREN_____.

NO. OF PEOPLE RESIDING AT PLACE OF EVENT:_____.

NO. OF PEOPLE WITNESSING THE EVENT:_____.

NAME OF OTHER PERSON WHO WITNESSED EVENT:
#1_____.   RELATIONSHIP_____.   AGE _____.
NAME OF OTHER PERSON WHO WITNESSED EVENT:
#2_____.   RELATIONSHIP_____.   AGE_____.
NAME OF OTHER PERSON WHO WITNESSED EVENT:
#3_____.   RELATIONSHIP_____.   AGE _____.

OTHER WITNESSES BY NAME AND AGE:
_____
_____.

WERE ANY PETS PRESENT? (if yes, explain):_____
_____.

DATE(S) EVENT(S) OCCURRED:_____
_____.

APPROXIMATE TIME(S) EVENT(S) OCCURRED:_____
_____.

WEATHER CONDITIONS PRESENT:_____
_____.

BRIEFLY DESCRIBE THE EVENT:_____
_____

DESCRIBE YOUR FEELINGS AT THE TIME OF THE EVENT:_____
_____.

IN WHAT ROOM(S) DID/DOES THE EVENT OCCUR?:_____
_____.

DESCRIBE FURNISHINGS IN THE ROOM(S) WHERE THE EVENT(S)
OCCURRED_____.

APPROXIMATE DURATION OF EVENT:_____

_____.

HAVE EVENTS OCCURRED BEFORE? (IF YES, BRIEFLY EXPLAIN):_____

_____.

HAVE THE EVENTS INCREASED IN FREQUENCY? (IF YES, BRIEFLY EXPLAIN):

_____.

DO YOU KNOW THE HISTORY OF THE PLACE? (IF YES, BRIEFLY EXPLAIN):

_____

_____.

DO YOU KNOW THE NAME OF THE PRIOR OWNER(S)?:_____

_____.

IF YOU CAN, DRAW WHAT YOU SAW IN THIS BOX.

Please return this questionnaire to *G-Host Publishing,*
Robert Wlodarski and Anne Wlodarski
8701 Lava Place, West Hills, California 91304-2126
Phone/Fax: 818-340-6676 · E-mail: robanne@ix.netcom.com

(Thank you for your time and patience in completing this form)

PHOTOGRAPH RELEASE FORM

If you've experienced anything out of the ordinary, something unexplainable, or an event that might be considered paranormal while visiting a restaurant, tavern, inn, or hotel, we would love to hear from you by enclosing this form as well as the following, Documenting Your Event form for possible inclusion in revised additions of this book. We would appreciate only first-hand experiences, and if you have them, and photographs taken of the event. Once again, if you would like your story told, please fill out the enclosed release form, and documenting your event form, and send it to the address below. If your story or photograph is used, we wish to provide proper you with the proper credit. If you wish to remain anonymous, please fill out the forms with the correct information, then attach a brief note stating you wish you wish to remain anonymous.

SEND TO

G-HOST PUBLISHING
Robert Wlodarski and Anne Wlodarski
8701 Lava Place, West Hills, CA 91304-2126
Phone/FAX: 818-340-6676
E-mail: robanne@ix.netcom.com

I hereby grant to **G-HOST Publishing**, permission to reproduce the attached material and/or photographs I have supplied for inclusion in revised editions to Southern Fried Spirits, or other subsequent publications dealing with ghosts and the paranormal.

I further consent to the publication and copyrighting of this book to be published in any manner G-HOST Publications may deem fit.

Proper acknowledgment of my photograph(s) material(s) will be provided by G-HOST Publishing within the context of the publication at the publisher's discretion.

Your name: _____

Your address: _____

Your phone number: _____

Date of submission: _____

Signature: _____

THE HAUNTED QUEEN MARY

Long Beach, California

ORDER FORM:

Please send me_____copies of *A Guide To The Haunted Queen Mary*. The purchase price is <u>$11.95</u> (DO NOT SEND CASH). To order by mail, please add the following:

* For postage and handling in the United States, please add <u>$3.20</u> for each book, (allow 3-4 weeks for delivery).
* All California residents add <u>$.99</u> / book to cover sales tax.
* For Foreign orders (including Canada) add <u>$5.00</u> for postage and handling.

You may also purchase the book on board the Queen Mary, or ask your favorite bookstore to order it for you.

U.S. Orders: $11.95 x no. of copies = $_____

Shipping (U.S.): $3.20 x no. of copies = $_____

Shipping (Foreign): $5.00 x no. of copies = $_____

Sales tax (California only): $.99 x no. of books = $_____

                              TOTAL ENCLOSED $_____

SEND CHECK OR MONEY ORDER (U.S. FUNDS) TO:

Send Check or Money Order (U.S. Funds) To:
GHOST PUBLISHING
8701 Lava Place, West Hills, California 91304-2126
Phone/Fax: 818-340-6676 - E-mail: robanne@ix.netcom.com

MAIL MY BOOK(S) TO:

Name:_____

Address:_____

City:_____

State:_____ Zip Code:_____

Phone Number (   ) _____

SPECIAL OFFER

BUY ANY OTHER GHOST BOOK DIRECTLY THROUGH
G-HOST PUBLISHING
USING THIS ORDER FORM AND TAKE $2.00 OFF!

THE HAUNTED QUEEN MARY	$13.95*	$11.95*
HAUNTED ALAMO	$12.95*	$10.95*
HAUNTED CATALINA	$12.95*	$10.95*
HAUNTED ALCATRAZ	$13.95*	$11.95*

*SHIPPING AND HANDLING: INCLUDE $3.00 PER BOOK

ORDER ALL FOUR BOOKS FOR $39.95 - SHIPPING AND HANDLING $7.50

Send Check or Money Order (U.S. Funds) To:
G-HOST PUBLISHING
8701 Lava Place, West Hills, California 91304-2126
Phone/Fax: 818-340-6676 - E-mail: robanne@ix.netcom.com

MAIL MY BOOK(S) TO:

Name:_____

Address:_____

City:_____

State:_____ Zip Code:_____ Phone Number_____